# Public Land Elk Hunting

By Matthew Dworak

Public Land Elk Hunting

© Copyright 2013

Published by Matthew Dworak

http://dirtysdealings.com/

ISBN-13: 978-1492176992

ISBN-10 11492176990

## Dedication

To my wonderful wife Wendy, who encourages me to pursue my passions while somehow managing to keep the home fires burning in my absence. There is no way I could do what I do without her support. I know that doing the work of two while I'm away chasing elk is no easy task. She is my greatest friend and my rock.

To my dad, who introduced us to the great outdoors. Whether it was chasing small game or bluegills with a cane pole, he always took the time to bring his sons and their friends along and was more concerned about passing along a tradition than bagging a trophy. If I can be half the role model to my two sons that he is to me, I'll consider myself lucky.

To all the others who have inspired, taught, packed, and sweated with me in this addiction we call elk hunting, I can't wait to do it all over again!

## About the Author

Matt Dworak is a Colorado native and was first introduced to elk hunting as a young child when he joined his father on his annual elk hunting trips. At that time, he and his brother Andy (Drew) could barely see above the shrubs as their father called in elk, they were both quickly infected with the elk bug. It is a passion that has carried on throughout Matt's life. Father of two young boys, Beau and Barrett and married to the love of his life, Wendy. Mr. Dworak spends his days working in a mechanical engineering firm designing building mechanical systems and daydreaming about upcoming hunting seasons.

The author is active in the Colorado archery community and serves as the president of the Fort Collins Archery Association, a life member of the Colorado Bowhunters Association, as well as many other conservation groups. He has been actively chasing elk for over twenty years.

The Next Generation

# Table of Contents

# Preface

Every year, I talk with hunters who shake their heads while explaining the various reasons they didn't fill their tags. Considering that we were "those guys" for many years, I want to do anything I can to help them become more successful; over the years, we've learned several things that have unequivocally improved our success rate in the field.

This book is not intended for the seasoned veteran; rather, it was written for the hunter who either isn't having much "luck" or has always dreamt of heading out west but doesn't know where to start. While many books have been written on the topic of trophy elk hunting, I haven't seen much dedicated to the regular guys/gals who are hunting on public land and consider any animal, bull or cow, a prize. But it's exactly that public land hunt where we feel most at home!

I'll be the first to admit that there are many who are much more successful than I could ever imagine being, who haven't had to go through so many years of trial and error before finally putting all the pieces together. But for all those successful hunters, I know there are many more who are still looking for all the stars to align, and these are the guys I'm hoping to help.

The results of a great public land hunt!

# Introduction

Life, in this day and age, is more complicated than ever. We live in the Information Age, and while that can be convenient, it can also be overwhelming at times. For the people who are just getting started, game regulations and drawing applications can be too complicated, but it doesn't have to be. If you like to hunt whitetails in the back forty, there's no reason why you can't be successful hunting elk. Do the research, set the tent up in the back yard, get your bow/rifle sighted in, enlist some buddies to split fuel costs, and never look back!

But why a book? Why do we need a book on elk hunting, if so much other information is so readily available? I struggled with this question for a while. Do people even read books in this electronic age? I know I do, and sometimes it's nice to have all the basic information in one place, without the need for a cord or a Wi-Fi connection. We have an unlimited supply of information right at our fingertips wherever we turn, but we still need to understand the basics before looking for the details. My intent with this book is to provide you with that understanding, and once you have a grasp on the basics, you can turn to the last chapter for a list of various online resources that I feel are worth mentioning.

In fact, those online forums were basically the catalyst for this book. After spending more time than I'd care to admit on the hunting forums, I noticed that the same questions are being asked over and over again. That trend made it apparent to me that the basic building blocks are missing for more than a few individuals, and the most frequently asked questions really helped shape what is included on the following pages. As valuable as all of this is, let me remind you that this is only the first step. I highly recommend seeking know-how from a variety of sources: printed media, audio, and online forums to further enhance your elk education.

# The Trifecta

We had bow hunted elk for many years, but we had little to show for it, other than overflowing bowls of tag soup. While all those experiences taught us many things, killing elk wasn't one of them. I can count on one hand the things that really made a difference in the outcome of our trips: find the elk, understand what is happening when you "get into elk"; and, when presented with a shot, make it count. While this all sounds very obvious, the dismal success rates across the west tells me that it's not coming together for the majority of hunters. When we first started making the transition from seldom filling tags to expecting to fill them, we decided that there is, in fact, an elk hunting "trifecta," a generic term for the breakdown of the three basic ingredients of a successful elk hunt in the field. The basic concept is that elk hunting success depends on three factors: shooting, elk vocalization and behavior, and physical conditioning.

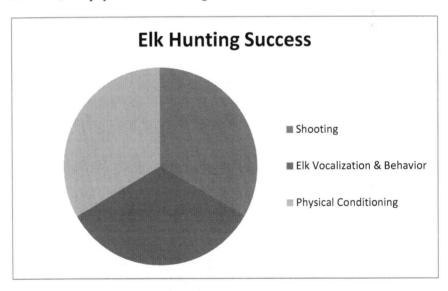

**Shooting** – This is the most obvious factor in determining your overall success, as you will not kill elk if you cannot make the shot, period. You work much too hard in the elk woods not to be able to capitalize on any opportunity when it presents itself. Imagine being five days into a tough elk hunt, hunting hard every day through unforgiving weather that has left you cold, wet, tired, and with no sign of elk life. Then, all of the sudden, everything magically comes together for that once-in-a-lifetime opportunity, but only for just a few short seconds. Your reaction HAS to come automatically. This is where time at the range over the summer or a year-round shooting regimen comes into play. This is also the only variable you can control while elk hunting. Weather, elk movement, hunter pressure, fires, and domestic stock grazing are out of your control, but your shooting is not. You must be able to make it count when the opportunity presents itself!

**Vocalizations & Behavior** – Understanding what the animals are doing and why is key to becoming regularly successful in the field. One of the biggest challenges we faced when we first started hunting elk was finding the critters to begin with. Hunting the vast expanses of land in the west is hugely different than hunting whitetails in the back forty. Elk can travel miles every day, moving from feeding to bedding areas; this is the best-case scenario. All bets are off once they've been pressured or frightened by other hunters. While elk are much larger than that proverbial needle in a haystack, they can be just as difficult to find in their woodland home. What you do have going for you is that these needles have a tendency to let you know where they are. Sometimes these bugles are unprovoked, and other times, it takes a little coaxing. We'll discuss various methods to help narrow down your search in later chapters.

**Physical Conditioning** – While I wish I could say there are ways to get around this one, in all honesty, being successful in public land elk hunting requires hard work. Sure, some elk hot spots don't require miles of backcountry walking, but those are far more the exception than the rule. Even if you're fortunate enough to know some close-to-the-road honey holes, elk are big, heavy critters that don't come out of the woods easy once they hit the ground. You must be in sufficient shape to maneuver through the woods, as well as deal with an animal once it's down. In my experience, those little seeds of doubt in the back of your mind can really have a negative impact on your overall success. If you start to wonder, *Can I really get an animal out from way back here?* you may as well turn around and start hunting closer to the truck. I like going into the season knowing that I'm going where the elk are, and if I've done my best to prepare myself for the hunt, those little seeds of doubt don't have a chance to grow.

While every factor in the trifecta is important on its own, balance is equally important; in fact, it is essential. You may be the top shooter in your local 3-D league, but if you're not in sufficient physical condition come September, that supreme marksmanship won't do you any good. Conversely, if you're running ultra-marathons but neglecting to shoot your bow, chances are good that you'll fail come crunch time. As with many things in life, it's all about balance.

## Basic Woodsmanship

We should never take for granted the little things we were taught as kids when our fathers took us into the field; not everyone is fortunate enough to have had such personal exposure and education. For this reason, I'd like to share some of the basics that I learned early on.

Typically, many subconscious things happen while hunting. Most things I do when in the woods occur automatically, so it's an interesting exercise to actually make a mental note of why we do what we do while walking through the woods: what we're looking at, what we're hearing, and what smells waft into our nostrils.

I never feel quite as alive as when my feet hit the forest floor in the elk woods and all my senses awaken. There's not a smell, sight, or sound that goes unnoticed, and this awakening is why I cherish any time spent in the woods so much.

**Use your eyes.** As you start your walk into the woods, whether it's down a well-worn trail or bushwhacking through the forest, keep your head up. It requires a certain comfort level to walk through the woods without watching your feet, but after a while, this will become second nature. You'll be amazed at what you've been missing. It also forces you to slow down. You're in the elk woods after all, and you really don't have any other place to be.

**Use your ears.** This doesn't just encompass hearing that bull scream from the meadow; nobody is going to miss that. I'm talking about all the other sounds that will surround you: birds singing, squirrels barking, chipmunks stirring, and crickets chirping. These sounds (or lack thereof) can tell you what's happening, even if it's out of your range of sight. Did everything suddenly go quiet? Why did that squirrel start chirping like crazy? Pay attention to your surroundings with all of your senses, including your ears; that might just give you a few precious seconds of warning before something is about to happen.

**Use your nose.** The first time I stalked up on an elk going solely off of smell was a day I'll never forget. Along that same vein, I also vividly remember the first time I noticed the wind do a 180 while I was still hunting through a bedding area and all the elk erupted out in front of me. Elk have a very pungent odor, something like the elephant enclosure at your local zoo. When you smell it, you'll recognize it immediately. Use this to your advantage. If you're walking down a trail or through the woods and hit a wall of elk stink, stop! Notice from which way the wind is blowing. Chances are, if you smell an elk, one is nearby or has been nearby recently. Either way, you've stumbled across something useful, so pay attention and don't walk aimlessly past.

## Elk Hunting 101 Vocabulary

**6x6** – Describes the number of points on each side of the antlers. A bull with four points on one side and five on the other would be considered a 4x5.

**Bivy** – From the word bivouac, means to carry camp, food, clothes, hunting gear, everything needed to survive on the mountain on one's backs.

**Branch-Antlered bull** – Describes any bull larger than a spike, whose antlers have split, resulting in more than one point.

**Brow Tine** – The first antler point closest to the skull.

**Broadside** – Refers to the position of the animal when it is perpendicular to the shooter.

**Bull** – A male elk.

**Calf** – A first-year elk.

**Cow** – A female elk.

**Herd Bull** – A mature bull with cows. While the herd bull will maintain control over a group of cows, this does not always mean he is the biggest bull on the mountain. He will, however, be the meanest!

**Quartering To/Away** – Quartering to is when an animal is facing the shooter at an angle of roughly forty-five degrees. Quartering away is the opposite, where the rear of the animal is facing the shooter at an angle.

**Raghorn** –This term means different things to different people, but in general, it is used to describe lesser, immature bulls, ranging from spikes to four- or five-point animals.

**Rub** – The place where a bull elk has raked his antlers across the bark of a tree either to remove the velvet or as a display of dominance.

**Rut** – The breeding season for elk. This occurs annually, when the cows are responsive to breeding, typically the third and fourth weeks of September.

**Spike** – A bull elk with a single point.

**Satellite** – A lesser bull that circles the herd, hoping to sneak off with a cow when the herd bull is distracted; hence their name, as they are continually circling like a satellite does around the Earth.

**Sign** – A generic reference to any evidence an animal has been in the vicinity, tracks, droppings, displaced vegetation, rubs, etc.

**Tag** – Hunting license.

**Velvet** – The fuzzy covering that appears on antlers when they grow in the spring and summer. Velvet is shed around mid-September, as the antlers harden prior to the rut.

**Wallows** – A springy, seeping, or wet, muddy spot in which a bull elk urinates and rolls around to cover himself with mud/urine. This mud/urine mixture helps the bull advertise his scent.

## Wind

Wind is so important in relation to elk hunting that it could have its own chapter. Especially when bow hunting, you'll never harvest anything unless you pay close attention to which way it's blowing, swirling, and shifting. You should notice it as you walk around town, and it should always register in your brain. I guarantee the elk's thinking about it!

**Thermals**

Thermals describe the basic pattern wind follows on a daily basis. Each morning, as the land begins to heat, the warm air surrounding the land begins to rise; conversely, toward evening, as the land mass cools, the surrounding air begins to fall. Understanding this basic principle can be helpful when planning a hunt strategy or stalking. Many hunters start at the top of a mountain early in the morning and work their way down mid-morning, capitalizing on the thermals bringing heated air upslope and keeping the wind in their face. In this way, they're continually working into the wind.

Thermals are more pronounced in steeper terrains, and it's been my experience that the evening thermals, flowing downslope, are more pronounced than the morning thermals. The morning air does not follow the terrain as it heads straight up, but as that air cools in the evening, it moves across the ground, flowing like a river. As you work up a steep drainage in the evening, you'll notice how the wind direction can change significantly as sub-drainages merge with the main drainage, much like tributaries in a river.

Vegetation

While this is by no means a comprehensive field guide to trees and shrubs, I thought it might be useful to include several select photos of some typical habitats encountered in elk country. At a minimum, these may be useful while talking with others who give you landmark-oriented directions: "Drive down the valley until you hit the draw with the Oak Brush." If you don't know what Oak Brush is, you may not take as much from such a conversation.

Lodgepole Pine with Vaccinium undergrowth

Pinyon Pine

Aspen foreground, Gambel Oak (Oak Brush) far hillside.

Gambel Oak (Oak Brush)

Our father always encouraged us to stay out all day, a lesson I'm grateful for. If you're accustomed to a morning hunt, then making your way back toward camp for a big breakfast and siesta, I'd highly encourage you to rethink your regimen. Here are a few reasons why:

- Other hunters push game as they are walking back after the morning hunt.
- It's almost a guarantee that you'll never kill anything while in camp.
- It takes more energy to walk back and forth than to just pull up a comfortable seat for the day.

While it's true that elk are most active at first and last light, sitting in camp for the rest of the day doesn't necessarily make a lot of sense. After the elk have been out feeding at night and make their way back to their bedding areas to relax and digest their food, there may be a little quiet time, but that doesn't mean the animals will sleep from ten to four. In fact, we've killed just as many animals during that midday downtime as we have during morning or evening hunts.

*Many struggle with what to do with themselves in the field all day. Personally, I keep a journal with me, and whenever I have a little downtime during the hunt, I make sure to take some notes.: how much game I've seen, mistakes I've made that I don't want to repeat, and gear that needs to be repaired, altered, replaced, purchased, etc. Being able to look back at past mistakes is a huge advantage to becoming a more successful hunter. Remember we only do this once a year, and it's tough to remember all those little nuances that are learned during the course of a season.*

Oftentimes, during the peak of the rut, bulls will continue to bugle all day. You must be in the right spot at the right time to hear that bugle so you can capitalize on the situation.

This is somewhat speculative, but there are several reasons hunters return to camp during the middle of the day. Some have been taught that it's the thing to do when elk hunting; it is a vacation, a chance to be away from the rigors of everyday home life and work, so filling a tag is not much of a concern. Winds can be more unpredictable at that time of day, which can be a valid excuse. My guess, though, is that most hunters simply don't know what to do with themselves in the woods for that amount of time. Here are a couple tips to keep you in the field where the action is.

- Take a nap. It isn't necessary to head all the way back to camp to take a quick snooze. You never know when you'll awake to the sounds of twigs snapping, and if you had the forethought to nock an arrow before your eyelids closed you might be able to fill your tag.
- Take snacks with you.
- Shoot a stump or grouse.
- Bring along a small packable rod/reel. Those high-county Brookies or Cutthroat can be a lot of fun!
- Do some light calling. It doesn't have to be anything crazy, but if you're sitting down for a snack, throw out a few low-volume cow calls. You never know what your noise-making might attract.

I'm not trying to sound like the elk Nazi here; in fact, it's just the opposite. For years, I wanted nothing more than to fill a tag, but somewhere along the line, I realized there's so much more to a great hunt. Once I started to relax in the woods, more often than not, something would materialize that wouldn't have had I been sitting in camp. The more time you spend in the woods, the more game you'll see, period.

### General Tips

In general, it comes down to always being prepared. If you're ready for any opportunity that might present itself, your chances of success will increase accordingly.

- Never leave your gun or bow out of reach! This is great, time-honored advice. When nature calls, you want to be sure you have your weapon with you; the last thing you want to do is to be caught with your pants down, so to speak!
- Always nock an arrow if you are going to sit down for any length of time, be it for lunch, coffee, or a short nap.
- My release goes on when the alarm clock rings and comes off after dark. If it gets in my way during the day, I tuck it into my shirt sleeve, but it never comes off.
- When setting up any type of ambush, be sure your bow is sitting in an upright position, with an arrow nocked. When an animal is in close proximity, lifting your bow off the ground and turning upright might prove to be too much movement.

- Stick to the shadows. When I'm in the woods these days, I feel like a vampire, because I rarely step into a brightly lit meadow, and I'll do whatever it takes to remain in the dark. If I'm covering ground to close the distance with an animal, I take a direct route, but if I'm sneaking around, it's always in the shadows.
- Be extra careful when crossing ridges, as your silhouette is much more visible than when you have a backdrop. Ridgelines are typically easier to navigate, and hunters often gravitate toward them, as it makes for easier walking and offers a clearer view, but don't be tempted into taking this route. A recent sheep hunt really emphasized the importance of this, as we'd routinely spot sky-lining game that we otherwise would not have seen.
- I'm not sure if "trailhead etiquette" is the right term for this, and it may seem like a complaint, but conversations at trailheads are always awkward. It isn't that I'm unfriendly, but typically, when I'm coming out the hills, I've been "into elk," and more often than not, those who hang around trailheads haven't. This may have something to do with strategy, but since one of my basic guiding principles is to tell the truth, when I'm asked, "Did you see any elk?" I have to say I have. Some ask for more information than that, expecting me to share info I worked hard to obtain, and I find that's where it get awkward. My best advice is to minimize time at the trailheads, at least for me it helps.
- To build off of the last point, I also never put much stock in what the trailhead groupies have to say. In general, they're a whiny bunch and typically very negative, commonly complaining: "It's too darn hot. We need some weather to get these elk talking. It's too dry. The moon is off. The elk are call shy. There are too many hunters," or even, "There are not enough hunters to move the game around." Don't buy it! I can't tell you how many times I've heard all these dire criticisms, but after a week in the hills and experiencing an amazing hunt, I just shake my head and load up as quick as I can. If you're heading in and hear any of these comments, don't pay them any attention. Just know that elk are out there doing what they always do, and it's up to you to find them.

## Tips from The Goat Ninja

This one is a little tricky for me to explain. After years of elk hunting together, I dubbed my brother "The Goat Ninja," because he has no problem going after elk, no matter what. What would intimidate most guys, like dropping down into a deep canyon or vertically climbing several thousand feet, doesn't bother my sure-footed, mountain goat-like brother for a second. When he hits the bottom of that dark canyon and the bull has already climbed to the top and bugles back down to him, he climbs right back out, without hesitation. If the bull bugles again from the bottom, The Goat Ninja is headed right back down there.

He also has an uncanny ability to silently sneak into the middle of a herd or ghost into the edges undetected. I don't know if it's because he's so fit and skinny that he can turn sideways and disappear, but like a ninja, he gets into situations I can't quite explain.

But what truly makes my brother my idol in the elk woods is that he never, ever gives up. When it comes to mental toughness, I'd put him up against anyone. I still recall some of our toughest elk hunts, when we were just cutting our teeth. Once, on the sixth day of a week-long hunt during which we haven't spotted a single critter, the alarm rang at four a.m. It had been raining steadily for the past several days, and our clothes had reached the point of saturation. When the alarm rang, I heard the raindrops pelting the tent and breathed a sigh of relief, glad we had a good excuse for sleeping in that morning. When I heard my brother pulling his pants on and zipping them up, I thought to myself, *You've gotta be kidding me!* At that point I really wasn't surprised when I heard him say, "Come on, Matt! Get your ass up!" The Goat Ninja is just plain salty!

When everyone else is huddled around the campfire, tucked under a tarp, trying to stay warm and dry, he has some of his best hunting days. The elk will do their thing, regardless of weather (within reason), and it seems they expect their pursuers to take a day off during inclement weather. What the elk don't count on is The Goat Ninja, my brother, being in their neighborhood. Drew actually enjoys stalking in wet, rainy conditions, when the leaves and sticks have been saturated, because sneaking around becomes a whole lot easier, and the sounds of a light rain make for a great cover. He also says the rain doesn't bother him because he'll end up sweating and damp anyway.

Now that you know why I admire The Goat Ninja so much, I'd like to share a little of the advice he's given me, some of the thoughts that run through his mind while working the woods:

The Goat Ninja At Work

## THE SUBCONCIOUS AND LITTLE THINGS

**Hilltops, Highpoints, Edges** – When creeping, always slow down or stop before cresting a hill or habitat edge (forest to meadow, etc.). Stuff always seems to be there, so be ready.

**Final Approach, Rubs** – When trying to move in close for a shot on a bull, wait for him to start thrashing a tree (if he has been already) to make quick five- to ten-yard moves. He can't see, and he's making a lot of noise. Also on the final approach, figure out the wind. Put any hills, drainages, trees, or rock outcroppings between you and the elk. There is no reason you can't get a lot closer with one of these beauties to hide you.

**Stopping Elk for a Shot** – Have a diaphragm in your mouth when you know you're close. Try a quick cow call or pop-n-grunt to stop an elk in your shooting window. I like to wait until I see their full head enter my window, since it seems to take about one full step for them to stop. If you're already sighted in, you can release the arrow as soon as the elk stops.

**Drawing Your Bow** – Remember, you may have to hold it for a while if you draw too early, but if you draw too late, you might get busted from moving or making a sound. This definitely depends on the specific situation, but at what seems to be my average shots (forty to forty-five yards), I like to draw when the elk is ten to fifteen yards from where I'm hoping to shoot it. I always wait for its head to go behind something first, if possible. If it is going to be a closer shot (ten to twenty yards), you almost have to draw when the elk is twenty-plus yards from where you hope to kill it. If you wait too long, the odds of getting busted seem to go up with every step the elk makes toward you.

**Rain** – This can be a blessing in disguise. I love creeping in the rain, since it makes my footsteps quiet and drowns out a lot of sounds. It's great for getting in close.

**Sitting** – If I'm going to sit down for any reason, I always clear every leaf, twig, and pinecone from my area and a few feet around any tree or obstacle I'm sitting next to. Then I can get on my knees, slide for a better shot, or take a few steps to get a better shot without making unnecessary noise. I also take a GPS point immediately in case I need to make a quick move for something farther away. That way, I can grab my bow and shove my GPS in my pocket and worry about my other gear later, without worrying about losing it. Of course, always nock an arrow before sitting and ducking into a bush for number-two. I've been burned on this one before.

**Bugling** – If the elk are not bugling, it doesn't hurt to throw one out at them for a potential response. I like to do so every quarter-mile if I'm moving somewhat fast or far. If a bull responds, I will sprint in that direction to try and close the distance as quickly as possible. The fewer sounds I make now (bugles, cow calls, etc.), the better. Hopefully, I'll find the elk, or he'll sound off again so I can lock in on his position. If hunting with a buddy, your partner can hang back and keep the bull talking. This is deadly!

When trying to locate a random bugle, I like to do little squeals and moaning-sounding bugles during the day. It seems that the majority of the bugles I hear in the mornings and evenings are the long, crisp locate bugles we all like to hear. In the daytime, however, I seem to hear more squeals or moans, like a big bull is lying around yawing or just making noises like my dog likes to do.

With bugling, if possible, be on top of a bowl or drainage so you can move fast to a responding elk. It's a lot easier to go down than up, although the elk will probably eventually make you go up, down, and up again.

When bugling, remember other sounds that are often made by elk (non-vocalizations). Stomping and raking trees adds a lot of realism when you're trying to sound like a fired-up bull. I like doing this with or without a bugle.

**Being Ready (Bugling, Cow Calling)** – Always nock an arrow before throwing out any elk call. If I did this diligently and had been ready for an elk to step out of the closest group of trees (forty yards) as he responded with a challenging bugle with grunts, I would have killed him. I had to stay still for several minutes and watch him turn back into the trees before I could draw.

Not only did I not know he was there, but I also found out he had about thirty cows with him.

**Elk Urine** – In my opinion, if you see a wet spot and confirm it is elk piss, there is an elk very close. Droppings seem to stay wet or fresh longer than piss. The last time I saw fresh piss and let my guard down, Matt and I blew a small herd out from a bedding area a few minutes later.

**Elk Sightings** – If I see an elk that looks to be alone, I always assume it is not. There always seems to be another cow or bull behind the one I'm looking at, and that one could bust me if I make a move too quickly without finding out how many eyes might be watching me.

**Trails and Rubs** – If I'm trying to cover some ground to find elk, I usually try to find a game trail or open forest. If I'm on a trail and see a lot of rubs, I slow down and get off the trail. It seems that the bull(s) making the rubs are doing the same thing so I start looking for them.

**Aspen Forests** – If I'm hunting in aspen, I check the little pockets of dark timber that always seem to be around. Even if I don't find an elk, I usually find a rub, a skeleton, or some elk droppings. It seems they like these spots, probably for shade, so they're worth checking out.

**Go Where the Sign Takes You** – When I'm creeping in the woods, I love the fact that I have nowhere to be and no time constraints, other than sundown. If I find any sort of sign, whether it's fresh droppings or even just a gut feeling that comes from the ways things look, I follow it until I find some more or feel like it's not happening. Then I can just move on, and it never hurts to check.

**Time Constraints** – If you're hunting with a bivy or something that allows you to sleep where you want, there are no time constraints, in my opinion. If you find elk and the sun is about to set, get out of the way, sleep with them, and kill them first thing in the morning. This is the only way to go, in my opinion, and if you're lucky, you'll go to sleep and wake up to a bugling forest.

**Creeping** – I think this one just comes to you when you're doing it, but a few things come to mind. Creeks and riparian areas can be good or bad. If they are shallow drainages, they usually have soft edges with soft grasses to walk on, which is great. On the other hand, a lot of the riparian areas in the forest have large-leafed plants that tend to be noisy when you're walking through them or trying to get out of them. Because of the running water, it is hard to hear anything else, including bugles and cow calls. Although the creeks may seems to be a quiet, easy route, stay 50 to 100 yards above or below so you will be able to hear and have room to maneuver without making extra noise.

I like to keep my diaphragm in my mouth so if I do get into something that causes me to make a lot of noise, I can mew a few cow calls and hope to trick something into not blowing out of the country.

**Bivy Camp** – Try to camp by water. If you're moving out in the morning, remember to use creek water for all boiling purposes, such as dinner and coffee, and save your iodine pills. Speaking of pills, 1980 called, and they want their heavy backpacking water filters back.

Another thing I like to do is fill my Jetboil with morning coffee water the night before. Then I ignite it in the morning and pack up camp while my coffee/breakfast brews. It saves precious time.

When trying to find a bivy spot where there doesn't appear to be any, try to remember that the spot only needs to be the size of your body. I had to keep this in mind when sheep-hunting with the mini-tent. There were a few nights where the tent didn't set too level, but there was a depression in the middle that I could fit into.

I like to wad up a couple plastic grocery bags in my pack for trash. I usually accumulate a lot of Mountain House trash, and they can get everything messy in your pack if you're not careful.

**Alarm Clock** – I always think waking up won't be a problem, especially considering I'm probably going to be sleeping in an uncomfortable position. Still, I've slept in before, and it felt like I'd wasted a whole day (prime time anyway). Bring a small alarm clock, watch, or phone you can rely on.

**Gear** – Obviously, be proficient with all your equipment. Keep things quiet. Self-adhesive felt is great and essential for arrow rests, bow limbs, clunky binoculars, rangefinders, or pack buckles, etc.

**Detachable Daypack** – I always have a small pack on or within my big pack that has the essentials to get through a day after killing an elk. This holds my GPS (if it's not tethered to my waist or in my pocket), a headlamp, water, one meal and a few snacks, a bugle tube, Paracord, and game bags. Knives are already on my side, and diaphragm is in my mouth or pocket. Whether my bivy camp is already set up and I'm going out to hunt within a few miles for the day or I'm temporarily dropping my big pack to investigate something, I always grab my small pack; if I see an elk, though, it's just the bow and GPS.

That way, I know I can go after elk if I find some, kill and process the elk and take care of the meat, and have food, water, and light to get back to my camp.

**Map and Compass** – I love GPS units and use them often, but I always have a map of my area and a compass in my pocket. Note that none of these do any good if you don't know how to use them, at least in a basic sense.

**Blood Trails** – Never stop looking for blood, but also remember the other things that might give you a clue: broken branches, bent-over grass and vegetation, out-of-place rocks, sticks, or logs, direction of travel, easiest paths, and the nastiest stuff to crawl into and die, etc.

**Caring for Meat** – Make it happen! Game bags are essential. Paracord is perfect for holding a dead elk in position if you are cutting it up alone. It's also great for hanging quarters. If my scrawny ass can take care of an elk by myself, anyone can. In my opinion, you should always get the meat off the mountain first and worry about the antlers later.

## Reading Sign

Being able to determine if the tracks or droppings you're seeing are from hours ago or days ago is something that only comes with practice. There are many variables in an outdoor environment—wind, rain, sun, snow, etc.—that will change the appearance of both tracks and droppings over time. For instance, droppings deposited in the shade on a humid day will receive protection from the wind and will look fresher longer than the same deposit left in an open meadow in full sun. This is where time in the field is required.

Cow Elk

I've included the following pictures to give the new hunter a starting place, to help you better understand what you're looking at when you hit the woods. First, the pointed edge tells the direction of travel; walk in the direction of the point. New tracks will have crisp edges. They will also be clean, with nothing in the track. For instance, when hunting in the snow, sometimes you'll find tracks, with discernible new snow within them, revealing that these were left prior to the last flurry.

Doe Deer

The tracks shown here are clear and easy to follow, but typically you won't be so lucky, as these were left under ideal conditions. Many times, you'll only be able to identify partial tracks, if they're even discernible. A bull track will be substantially larger than a cow's, and, depending on the age of the bull, the tracks can vary substantially in size. A young cow and a spike bull will have tracks similar in size. The main objective for the new woodsman is to be able to differentiate between deer and elk. Then, with time in the field, bull and cow, then between young bulls and old, but this is a skill that only develops with practice and firsthand observation.

Once you've seen enough tracks to confidently tell old from new, you've developed a very important skill. Whenever I'm walking the trail and "cut" new tracks, I take notice and know that if I follow them, it won't take long to find the animal that left them. Fresh tracks are always something I pay attention to.

## Droppings

Fresh droppings are something else I always take note of; if they're extremely fresh I can almost guarantee elk will be in the immediate area. Conversely, if they're old, I hardly pay any attention, since I'm interested in where the elk are, not where they've been. Fresh urine spots are also great indicators that elk are in the immediate vicinity.

New Droppings. Notice the Sheen.

Again, don't let recent weather conditions that have rehydrated the droppings fool you into thinking they're fresh. If they're missing the slimy appearance, I can almost guarantee they're too old to put much stock in.

Old Droppings. These pellets have dried and have begun to collapse in on themselves.

Navigation

Getting around in the mountains becomes second nature to the experienced hunter, but gaining that experience and understanding is something that comes over time. Navigation can be as simple as memorizing landmarks and using them to help you get from Point A to Point B. The problem with navigating in the mountains is that it can be difficult to see landmarks in the thick forest. When a storm rolls in, obscuring all visual clues, you'll wish you had a few backup options.

There are many different maps out there, and each has its own purpose. For the big picture, I use *The Gazetteer* by Delorme. These are great for getting you to your hunting spot, and each book offers maps for an entire state. Where these shine over traditional atlases is that they show county and forest service roads, land ownership (both Forest Service and BLM), major contour lines, and lakes and streams. These really are useful tools.

Regardless of which map you choose, there are a couple things to keep in mind:

1. Remember that property boundaries change hands, so having the most current map possible is always advisable. Even then, however, you can never trust it 100 percent.

2. Buy the right tool for the job. While *The Gazetteer* maps are great for looking at large areas, they don't provide the detail you'll eventually want.
3. Maps don't do you much good without a compass. Get one and learn how to use it, at least the basics.

Once I have an area somewhat narrowed down, there are a couple other maps I look for: *Forest Service* and *National Geographic Trails Illustrated*. These are great and offer greater detail than *The Gazetteer* maps but still cover a large enough area that you're not focusing in on a particular drainage or trailhead. Finally, once I've really got some areas nailed down, I pick up a couple *USGS 7.5-Minute Series* topo maps for the actual areas where I'll be hunting.

Technology has changed the way many navigate in the outdoors, and today almost all backcountry enthusiasts carry GPS units. There are a couple things to keep in mind when using a GPS:

*Know your gear!*

It was our first experience hunting in a wilderness setting, and we quickly learned that it was very different from the national forests we'd grown up hunting, when we'd walk until we hit a road and then work our way back toward camp. It really doesn't work like that when there are no roads!

We'd been out hunting all day, and we were pushing the limits of how late we could stay out before having to head back to camp. We weren't worried about it getting too dark because we had our new Garmin Etrex in hand. As we started making the trip back toward camp, the sky grew darker and darker. Since there wasn't much of a moon, we soon had to stop and pull out headlamps and our brand new GPS. We turned it on and aimlessly started following the little triangle around, and it quickly became obvious that things weren't looking good. Because we didn't know our gear, my brother and I had to snuggle on the mountain that night like two lovers, shivering until it was light enough to see that we were less than a quarter-mile from our tent. Since then, we've learned to use our equipment, and we now romp around after dark without a second thought.

While neither of us ever thought we were in any danger, it did teach us a couple valuables lessons. Know your gear and how to use it, be prepared if you get stuck on the mountain, and, most importantly, hunt with someone sexier than your brother, just in case you have to snuggle to keep warm!

1. Electronic devices can fail. Never rely solely on your GPS for navigation or to know where you are.

2. Always carry spare batteries. I use electrical tape to hold them together. A couple of taped batteries means they are fresh and intended for one use only.
3. To conserve batteries, I leave my GPS off unless I want to enter a waypoint.
4. We prefer to use Universal Transverse Mercator (UTMs) over latitude/longitude (lat./long.). If you prefer, make this change in the setup menu of your GPS. UTMs are marked more frequently on a map vs. the lat./long, so interpolating a point from your GPS is much easier if you use UTMs.
5. Beware of reception loss or interruption, which can occur due to snow, fog, or tree cover, especially for older models prone to lose track of satellites. Newer GPS units equipped with more sensitive quad-helix antenna are less prone to insufficient signal acquisition in adverse conditions.

*GPS Tip*

While global positioning systems and woodsmanship may not sit well with some, GPSes can be great tools if you know how to use them. I always make a point to mark the truck, camp, or any spot I plan to return to. I also mark any relevant finds while in the field, particularly wallows and downed elk. While I don't plan on doing an in-depth GPS how-to here, a great tip I've learned is to get your bearings from a waypoint, then work with your traditional compass.

First, mark your camp before you leave in the morning. When it begins to get dark and your travels have carried you miles away, instead of holding your GPS in front of you the whole walk back, looking like a lost person who's never stepped foot in the woods before, find the waypoint you're looking for, and locate the bearing you need to follow. Once you know the bearing, you can turn off the unit and start heading that direction. For instance, if it says camp is 168 degrees at a distance of 2.4 miles, (make sure your unit is set to magnetic in the setup menu), you can now shut off your GPS, look at your compass, and head toward 168 degrees for 2.4 miles. It's also helpful to locate noticeable landmarks at the bearing you're heading toward, such as mountain peaks, the moon, etc. You can always recheck your bearing as you go, using your GPS, but you should be able to stay within a degree or two without too much trouble or depleting your batteries. This technique saves batteries, time, and energy, and most importantly, you won't be staring at GPS the whole walk back.

## Evening Navigation

Sooner or later, you'll find yourself wandering around in the dark, either heading out in the morning or returning at night. It isn't a bad thing—just a reality of elk hunting. The most important thing to remember is that navigating at night takes

a lot longer, two to three times as long as it does in the daylight, given that you're bushwhacking and not walking a trail or road. There is also a high likelihood that you will be hungry and tired by that point. This is one of the main reasons I enjoy bivy-style hunting; hiking miles into a spot each day and back at night takes a lot of energy. Regardless of your preferred hunting style, you'll eventually find yourself moving around in the woods in the dark.

The most obvious challenge is illuminating your path. I always carry two light sources in my pack, a small headlamp and a small flashlight. Light is a necessity, so redundancy is fine in packing it. I like the headlamp for camp chores, fixing meals, skinning and butchering, and illuminating the ground while traveling. A small, high-output flashlight is great to cast to beam far ahead to help with choosing the easiest route, and it can save time while you are working through areas with lots of downed timber and keep you away from terrain that may be more treacherous than you're looking for late at night. I've been carrying a Fenix PD30 that I love. It's small and lightweight and puts out a tremendous amount of light. It still amazes me something so small could make my old two D-cell Maglight look like a toy. My only hesitation in recommending it here is that it's not American made, which may be of importance to some.

## Creating a Waypoint

Imagine spending your evening glassing and finding elk feeding on a distant hillside. You know it's much too far for you to get to that evening, but you're sure you can get a crack at them if you can be there at first light.

Assuming it's an area you've never hunted before and you aren't sure if you can find the spot in the dark, just pull out your handy topo map and carefully locate the spot on the map. Next, grab your GPS and create a waypoint. Once the waypoint is created, you can edit its location. Very carefully enter the UTMs of location and verify it by using "Go to...waypoint" and making sure the bearing and distance sound accurate. If it tells you the spot is eighty-four miles in the opposite direction, you'll need to verify that you entered the location units correctly. Now you can start your hike in the pitch dark the next morning and reach your destination by legal shooting light.

## Campfires

To have or not to have, that is the question. There is no good answer to this one; our personal preference is to keep campfires to a minimum, though many hunters might disagree. Since most of our time is spent bowhunting, scent control is always on our minds, and while there isn't a lot that can be done at times in a backcountry environment, getting drenched by smoke doesn't seem to be a great idea.

I would never hesitate to build a fire if I or someone in the party needed additional warmth, but burning one just to roast weenies and marshmallows isn't something I prefer to do. I've heard the argument many times that smoke is natural and doesn't bother the elk, and some even purport that it's a great cover scent. These statements have never made any sense to me. The odor of humans is also natural, yet elk do not like it. Smoke can be an alarming aroma, and if humans assume that where there's smoke, there's fire, I'm relatively certain that elk also pay special attention to the out-of-the-ordinary, pungent odor of burning wood.

I should also add that rifle hunters can probably get away with a little more in regard to scent, as they don't work in such close quarters, but I personally still try to keep it to a minimum.

## Mountain Safety

I almost hesitated to include this section because I feel too many would-be elk hunters let the thoughts of the big, bad mountains scare them off before they ever step foot in them. While hunting the high country can have its risks, it is really no more dangerous than traveling along any busy highway; statistically, it's actually much safer. If you act in a reasonable manner and prepare your body and mind before the hunt, there's nothing to be worried about. However, since this book is geared more toward the novice, I'd be remiss if I didn't touch on the basics.

### Acute Mountain Sickness (AMS) or Altitude Sickness

AMS is caused by a sudden change in elevation, typically occurring above altitudes of 8,000 feet, where there is less oxygen. Those traveling to hunt are most susceptible to the symptoms of AMS, but those living at altitude must also be aware of the condition. More advanced cases of AMS can result in a high-altitude pulmonary edema (HAPE), a buildup of fluids in the lungs that may require hospitalization. High-altitude cerebral edema (HACE) can actually be life threatening.

### Symptoms of AMS or Altitude Sickness (HAPE or HACE)

- Headache
- Loss of appetite
- Nausea

- Fatigue
- Dizziness or lightheadedness

**Treatment for AMS or Altitude Sickness (HAPE or HACE)**

- If symptoms are detected, ascent should immediately be stopped, and a gradual descent should be planned.

The best way to avoid AMS is to make your ascent as leisurely as possible. When traveling from sea level, it's advisable to spend a day or two at a base elevation prior to making any strenuous climbs. Proper hydration is also key to staying healthy, and lots of water is your friend.

On a side note, just because you have previously hunted areas with no side effects, that doesn't mean you won't experience symptoms at some point, as physical changes occur within the body over time.

Medications containing Aceatzoamide (Diamox) can be prescribed by your doctor and should be taken before and during your trip. Wilderness Athlete also makes a product called Altitude Advantage that has received rave reviews.

I've been fortunate in that I've never experienced any altitude-related problems, but AMS is very real and affects thousands of hunters, hikers, and mountain climbers each year. Don't allow your hunt to be ruined or your health to be endangered due to poor planning and preparation. For more detailed information on AMS, please visit - http://www.ncbi.nlm.nih.gov/pubmedhealth/PMH0001190/

Weather
In the high country, weather can be one of your worst enemies. Here in Colorado, it's not uncommon for temperatures to remain in the eighties during the day but to drop to freezing at night. Throw in a few thundershowers or snowstorms, and you've got yourself a typical day in the mountains. Dressing in layers is the key to dealing with the constantly changing weather conditions. Mornings in elk camp will be cool to cold, so you should bundle up. Just 200 yards into your hike, you realize you no longer need your jacket. Adding or shedding layers becomes part of the routine. I will go into proper layering in greater detail later, but the key is to stay warm or cool and dry. One of the worst things you can do is to dress in thick clothing as you hike into your hunting spot, only to realize you're drenched in sweat. This has the potential to rapidly cool the body as the sweat evaporates, and this can be uncomfortable and harmful as your physical activity falls off.

## Hypothermia

One of the biggest threats to anyone spending time outdoors is hypothermia. In essence, hypothermia results when the body's core temperature cannot be maintained through regular metabolism, sending the victim into a downward spiral. The onset of hypothermia is usually brought on by cold coupled with moisture. Moisture can be in the form of rain, snow, or perspiration and causes an accelerated drop in the body's core temperature. Hypothermia is dangerous for any hunter because once the initial stages set in, the victim may not be able to think rationally and may not even be aware there is a problem.

### Symptoms of Hypothermia

- Severe shivering
- Loss of coordination, a sense of drunkenness, stupor

### Treatment for Hypothermia

- If the victim is unconscious, administer cardiopulmonary resuscitation (CPR).
- Remove any wet clothing.
- If possible, get warm fluids into the victim, such as tea, coffee, or clear soup.
- Elevate the core temp by placing the hypothermic individual in a heated vehicle, structure, or sleeping bag with other warm bodies.

## Dehydration

Staying properly hydrated is about as important as it gets. If you accidentally leave your canteen at camp or don't pack enough water, you'll quickly learn the importance of ample water for your body. The first step is to pack enough water, and the second is to make sure you have a backup plan in case you run out or your supply is ruined in some way.

- ✓ **Multiple Containers** – I always have a minimum of two, usually three, containers for water. I use a CamelBak or dromedary-type water system, approximately 100 ounces, a 32-ounce Nalgene, and a 16-ounce bottle to mix any powered drinks.

- ✓ **Water Purification Tablets** – Water treatment tablets such as Portable Aqua take up almost zero space in your pack and are safe and effective. We typically hunt in areas where the natural water supply is of high quality and rather clean, and we're pulling from clear streams and seeps, not mud puddles. If we were dealing with dirtier water, I'd pack a mechanical filter. One consideration when using the tablets is that you'll have to keep buying them, so, depending on the quantity of water you'll be treating, the use of a mechanical filter may make more sense.

✓ **Mechanical Water Filter** – There are a lot of good options on the market, though mine are mainly collecting dust. I've used an MSR for years with no complaints. I also pack a large, gravity-type filter, Katadyn Base Camp, when setting up a stationary base camp in the back county.

✓ **UV Light Treatment** – I have not used the SteriPEN but have heard nothing but good things about them. They use UV light to treat the water and will purify sixteen ounces in less than a minute or thirty-two ounces in less than two. I'd consider this over a mechanical filter because of the space and weight savings.

Drinking plain water for a week can get old. Here are a couple things I use to add a little variety to the routine:

- Propel
- Wilderness Athlete
- Emergen-C

These also help to mask the iodine flavor associated with some brands of tablets, and they also provide electrolytes and vitamins, both of which may be in short supply on a rigorous hunt.

### Lightning
Lightning is a regular occurrence in the high county. Unfortunately, hunters often find themselves miles from the truck when a storm hits, so running back to the rig is not an option. If you do find yourself in the middle of a lighting storm, your natural instinct may tell you to hide under a tree, but it is best to avoid isolated ones. Distance yourself from any metal objects (pack, bow, etc.) and sit in a crouched position, trying to balance on the balls of your feet. If you're above tree line, getting off the mountaintop should be a priority.

For more information regarding lightning safety, please visit NOLS Backcountry Lightning Safety Guidelines - http://rendezvous.nols.edu/files/Curriculum/research_projects/Risk%20Ma nagement%20Reports/NOLS%20Backcountry%20Lightning%20Safety%20G uidelines.pdf

---

## Predators

One of the most frequently asked questions is how a hunter should deal with bears and big cats. Statistically speaking, though, it doesn't need to be a main concern. The truth is, there are far more other, more prevalent dangers to concern yourself with, many of which I've already mentioned. The one exception is if you are hunting areas that have known grizzly populations; if you intend to hunt these areas, you should take every precaution to protect yourself.

I do not carry a sidearm while elk hunting because I cannot justify the extra weight for the areas we hunt in Colorado, but that is a personal choice, and many hunters feel more comfortable packing a weapon to defend themselves. If I were hunting big bear county, I would opt for pepper spray over a firearm, as it's been shown to be an effective deterrent against bears; studies have shown that individuals who deployed pepper spray were more likely to walk away from an encounter unscathed than those spraying lead. As with any other weapon, practice with pepper spray until you're comfortable deploying it. If you choose to carry a sidearm, whether a firearm or pepper spray, burying it in the bottom of your pack is about as good as leaving it on the counter at home. It needs to be in an accessible location where it can be immediately deployed if needed.

Hunters break just about every rule in the book when it comes to what to do in bear country, as we sneak silently around, imitating the sounds of the animals we're hunting. While running into bears and cats is certainly a possibility, every bear I've come across in the woods has turned tail and run. Only one didn't want to leave, which was a poor choice for the bear, as I just happened to have a tag in my pocket! If you do run into one, just remember to stand up tall, talk loud, and slowly back away, even if this is easier said than done. A confident, strong attitude can make a real difference when it comes to the animal kingdom.

Even though we break all the rules while in the field, we can keep a clean camp as much for ourselves as for the next camp after us and follow established guidelines in bear country. While I have heard some stories of big cats that make the hair on the back of my neck stand up, I can't think of a single one that actually ended badly.

## Communication

In our current Information Age, there's no excuse to be without reliable communication, even in the backcountry. Whether it's to talk to the other members of your hunting camp or the ability to contact the outside world in an emergency situation, communication should be covered in your preplanning for the hunt.

**Cell Phones** – Almost everyone has a cell phone these days, and with increasing tower coverage, it's easier and easier to get a signal the woods, although you'll typically need to climb to the highest point around. I keep an old non-Smartphone around for our annual elk hunt. I swap out SIM cards prior to heading out, and the battery on the old phone will last a week as opposed to the one-day charge on my Smartphone. You can also find spare batteries online for about five bucks, giving you the peace of mind that you'll have coverage your entire time in the field.

**Two-Way Radios** – These are great for keeping in contact with members of your camp while out in the field. One thing to keep in mind is that these devices work on line of sight, so rough or rocky terrain, hills, and trees will negatively affect your signal significantly. It's been my experience that a radio rated for five miles will typically work for about one mile in the mountains, and even that may be optimistic.

We prefer the Garmin Rhino, a two-way radio combined with GPS. These work great for the way we hunt, splitting up and reconvening later in the day or, in some cases, in the week. When used in conjunction with other Rhinos, the other user's location will update on your screen. This is great when hunters in a party take different routes but still want to stay in contact. This also comes in handy for hooking up once an animal hits the ground and a hunter needs some help.

**Satellite Phones** – Depending on the specifics of your hunt, a satellite phone may make great sense. Satellite phones will get coverage anywhere, as long as they have a clear view of the sky. Our annual hunt typically includes four or five guys, so renting a phone for a week is a very minimal expense. Currently, rental rates average about twelve dollars a day. Our normal hunting spot requires about an hour hike to the nearest peak where we can get a cell signal, and it's not an easy climb, so a few bucks for a week's rental is money well spent. Considering that we periodically check in with the family back home and call the packer with any updates, a satellite phone makes a lot of sense. The most important reason to carry a satellite phone is that it will come in handy in the event of an emergency.

**SPOT Satellite Messenger** – This unit has several unique features and should be considered by anyone who likes to wander off the beaten path. It is equipped with an SOS button, which will dispatch emergency responders to your exact location at a moment's notice. This can truly be a life-saving device. Current models also allow for minimal messaging (preprogrammed before you leave home) so folks at home will know you're doing all right. Those at home can also track your progress based on your GPS unit signal. Be aware that these devices require an annual subscription to utilize their services.

I should also mention that with any of these newer technologies, things are changing at a rapid pace. What's available today will likely be obsolete tomorrow. Nevertheless, you should have a solid communication strategy in place before heading into the field. Whether it's to stay in contact with loved ones or to be prepared for any necessary help or extraction in an emergency, having a reliable communication plan in place should be common sense.

# Physical Conditioning

An important factor in being comfortable in the woods is being able to get around without too much physical discomfort, and this preparation is something that should happen long before you head into the hills to hunt elk.

Think you're too old? This friend of ours killed his first elk at sixty-nine years young!

Some of my elk hunting heroes, Cameron Hanes and Dwight Schuh come to mind. These two take their conditioning to the next level by running ultra-marathons and performing other incredible feats. It certainly can't hurt, and attaining a higher level of physical fitness is always advisable, though you don't have to be an ultra-marathoner to be successful on an elk hunt. That said, I think that the outcome to any public land hunt is directly related to the amount of work put in, be it upfront planning/conditioning or physical effort in the field.

We often ask ourselves why we look forward to this all year-round, as we end up with bodies that are sore, bloodied, and bruised, but somehow we know it's worth it. We also know we're a little crazier and subject ourselves to a bit more than the average hunter, knowing that the more hills we climb and the farther we travel will result in higher dividends. If you put in the time preseason, you'll be that much more comfortable on your hunt; if you don't, you'll wish you did.

## Walking

If you've been less than active since graduating from high school, where do you start? That's easy! Just start walking! Nothing is simpler, and it produces results. You don't have to worry about a gym membership or injuries, and you won't be sore the next day. Walking allows you to strengthen your legs and cardiovascular system while also bringing your core into the picture, as something has to balance your torso while you're strolling down the street. Once you've developed a basic routine/route, change it up. Add some elevation or throw a little weight in a pack and vary your pace. It really is such a simple exercise and it is a great building block for any more advanced workout you may consider.

Another huge advantage of walking is that it conditions your feet. Make this a dual-purpose endeavor by breaking in those new hunting boots, a crucial aspect of any hunt. You'll be relying on your feet each day of the hunt, so getting your feet in trail condition and getting used to your footwear is critical.

Start small, with fifteen- to twenty-minute workouts. There's no need to dive into a rigorous routine that will likely make you really sore and derail your efforts. Make the commitment to work twenty minutes into your day, an easy amount of time for anyone to find in their hectic schedule. Just committing to this very basic regimen will help you lay the foundation for lifetime results, and even this minimal commitment will make you feel great. Before you know it, you'll be adding exercises to your routine, and your workouts will seem less and less intimidating.

**Hiking/Packing**

Once you've developed a comfortable base with your walking efforts, it's time to start working a little harder. Since the best way to train for an activity is to do it on a small scale, hiking with a pack in some rough terrain will do several things that will make your time spent in the woods more enjoyable. Firstly, you'll likely identify any deficiencies with your pack long before hitting the woods. Maybe your waist belt is too short and won't cinch down tight; it's far better to find that out at home than to discover it on your first 200 yards up the trail on opening morning.

The process will also get your entire body used to the extra weight. Your shoulders, core, legs, and feet will benefit from the training. Mentally, you'll know you're up to the challenges of the mountain, especially if you've worked your way up to packing fifty to seventy-five pounds. Don't give those little seeds of doubt a chance to grow!

## Other

If you'd like to continue to build off these basic routines, just keep in mind that your legs are what must get you to the top of the mountain and back again. If you're really looking for a greater challenge I'm a big fan of both P90x and Crossfit - http://www.crossfit.com/. Be warned, however, that you should not jump into these rather intense programs cold turkey; without a fundamental base knowledge, you may do more harm than good with these workouts. Both programs are scale-able, which means any fitness level can benefit from them, as you can adjust the repetitions, weights, times, etc. to suit your own fitness capabilities and needs.

For instance, the official Crossfit warm-up consists of the following: three sets, ten to fifteen reps each.

1. Samson Stretch
2. Air Squat
3. Sit-up
4. Back Extension
5. Pull-up
6. Dip

This could very well be a workout in itself. During times when I've fallen out of any exercise routine, I rebuild my foundation by doing this warm-up as my workout for the first couple of weeks.

If you are interested in Crossfit, I encourage you to seek out a local Crossfit facility, and I caution you to avoid the technical Olympic lifts in the beginning. Personally, I've suffered some setbacks in attempting the dynamic lifts without good coaching on basic technique.

Obviously, the choice is yours, and only you can decide whether or not you want to take on an exercise regimen. If you're serious about filling tags, though, it's rare for hunters to be successful without working out at some level prior to venturing into the wilderness.

# Mental Conditioning

I often wonder why I'm such an elk junkie. When I hear that bugle floating out from the valley floor one or two valleys over, I never stop to ask myself, "How far away was that?" I just start heading off in that direction. The problem is, when I arrive at that valley, I often hear another bugle, and off I go again. This scenario repeats itself throughout the day, until the sun finally sets and I have to consider where I am and how far it is back to camp. As I amble back, feeling the trekked miles of the day set in, with my feet feeling like they're made of hamburger, I often ask myself, "Why in the hell do I look forward to this all year?" The next thing I know, though, as soon as a bugle sounds, off I go again. Elk hunters take delight in the strangest things!

Nearly every elk or hunting book I've ever come across has contained a chapter on mental conditioning, so I considered leaving this information out, but there is good reason that so many resources are sure to cover this topic. Mental conditioning is absolutely critical to any successful hunt. In general, elk hunting is not easy. I tell newcomers to mentally prepare for a hunt that will basically resemble a week of basic training, as we don't exactly take it easy on our hunts, and I want them to show up expecting to be put through the wringer.

For me personally, mental preparation helps in almost every area of life. For instance, if I know I've got a work deadline looming that's going to require a sixty-plus-hour workweek and I have this information ahead of time, I give myself a pep talk, and it's not that big of a deal. If, however, that ominous information is thrown at me on Monday with a Friday deadline, I'll likely have a different attitude.

When it comes to elk hunting, I refer to the popular adage, "Prepare for the worst and hope for the best." Our minds do a wonderful job of saving only the highlights from past trips: when we called in that big bull, joking around the campfire with the fellas, or finally getting that shot opportunity and making it count. We tend to forget the more tumultuous and grim details: the miles walked, the no-sightings days, the freezing temps, the blisters and soreness, etc. We tend to romanticize things, to only recall the good times, but the reality is that elk hunting can be downright hard. Sure, we do it for fun, but that doesn't make it any less tough!

One of our good hunting buddies who hadn't been on a backpack/bivy hunt previously joined us for his first backcountry adventure last year. He was used to whitetail hunts, so I was a little nervous about how he'd do so far out of his comfort zone. To help him mentally prepare for the trip, I started sending him "Imagine this…" emails. For instance: "Imagine this…We're all piled in the truck, heading up into the hills, and everyone is in high spirits having a great time. After a while, the sky opens, and rain begins to fall. That rain quickly turns to snow. As we pull into the trailhead, there is about six inches on the ground, and by the time we make the five grueling miles back to camp, we're plowing through fourteen inches. To make matters worse, your canteen leaked in your pack, so most of your clothes and your sleeping bags are wet…"

This kind of scenario is very real, very possible, even though our minds might refuse to believe things could be so rough. If we force ourselves to accept the realities of the entire trip and properly prepare, we'll be much more ready to deal with any challenges we may encounter.

Our buddy ended up doing just fine on the trip, even though he didn't quite follow my advice on proper conditioning and we thought he might puke on the hike when he dropped to his knees and began to quiver on an exceptionally steep section of the trail, earning him the nickname "Preacher." I'm not sure he likes the nickname much, but I'd never seen anyone else doing any trail praying before.

## Confidence

A little confidence goes a long way in life, and it is no different when it comes to a hunt. If you go into it knowing you've done all you can to prepare, that positive attitude can significantly affect the outcome. You should be able to step out of the truck, suck in that fresh mountain air, and think, *Bring it on!* This is generally my mindset, because I know I've been physically and mentally preparing all summer. I've done my scouting and know I'll spot animals. My weapon is sighted in, and I have no doubt that I'll make good on any shot opportunity presented. I've been practicing my calling all summer and know any sounds coming out of my month will be spot on. I've packed my truck with all the necessities: coolers, game bags, ice, etc., everything I need to take care of an animal once it hits the ground. Nothing feels better than hitting the trailhead with confidence.

I probably spend more time getting into my own head than a lot guys, but there's nothing better than knowing I'm there to find my quarry and make a clean kill. The only thoughts in my head during the hunt revolve around how those two things are going to come together.

I've mentioned previously the importance of not allowing any seeds of doubt to sprout in your mind. There is very little you can control on the mountain, where you are at the mercy of Mother Nature, but you have a lot of control of the events leading up to that point. Use that to your advantage. It's difficult for those who have not yet killed an elk to understand how to get over that hurdle, but going into the hunt, knowing you're ready is a great first step.

**Mental Exercises**

Many prepare their minds and bodies with physical exercise. Not only will physical exercise strengthen muscles and endurance, but it will also boost your confidence; you will know you are mentally ready for the hunt. Just the act of getting off the couch for a workout is a hurdle that is difficult for some people to overcome. Once you've made the commitment to work out and follow through with that promise to yourself, your mental character will improve. Building upon the basic workout can help that much more.

A couple years ago, I signed up for the Steamboat Lake Sprint Triathlon. The race consisted of a half-mile swim, 12.4-mile bike ride, and a 3.5-mile run and took place at approximately 8,200 feet in elevation. This event was a fairly big deal to me. I hadn't done any swimming since high school, and I'm really not a big fan of jogging, so I couldn't help being proud when I finally crossed that finish line.

I learned some important things during that race. By signing up in the first place, I committed myself to getting in shape. Even though my

The Author coming Out of the Water after a Half-Mile Swim at the Steamboat Lake Spring Sprint Triathlon.

performance wasn't the greatest, I finished the race, and I was proud of myself for taking on the challenge. The only downside was that I felt like I was spending more time perfecting my swim stroke vs. getting dialed in at the range. In the future, I'll likely stick with lots of hiking to get in shape, but for some, participating in similar competitive events may be just the ticket. If nothing else, it absolutely helped get me in shape and build confidence, for I'd taken on something that had previously scared the heck out of me.

# Shooting

I am a projectile enthusiast. Whether it's an arrow, bullet, rock, or anything else, putting an object downrange, accounting for trajectory and wind drift, is something I've loved since I was a little kid. For me, shooting is fun, and it doesn't matter what the projectile is.

No matter what your preference is, be it rifle, muzzleloader, or bow, being confident in your ability to hit what you're aiming at is critical for a successful hunt. A lot of hunters get lulled into thinking they are a good shot and do not practice, only to realize when they get on the mountain, *Boy, it has actually been quite a while since I've shot old Betsy*, followed by, *I can't quite remember how far exactly she drops at 250 yards...and did I go to a heavier bullet?* This kind of second-guessing is a sure-fire recipe for unfilled tags. Building confidence obviously starts months in advance, and there are no shortcuts. You need to put in the time at the range to ensure that your weapon is properly sighted in. You must know where you're hitting at various ranges, and, just as importantly, you must be familiar enough with it that it becomes second nature to nock an arrow or chamber a round.

I can't emphasize enough the mental aspect of pulling off a shot in the heat of the moment, when that big bull is screaming in your face, your heart's racing, and that fresh shot of adrenaline slams into your bloodstream. Being able to pull off the shot at clutch time will determine if you'll be packing out meat or going home hungry.

Since we generally hunt with archery equipment, I've asked Zach Sanders, former recon Marine and law enforcement professional, current killing machine, and a good buddy of mine, to offer some advice. The remainder of the information in the rifle section was provided by Mr. Sanders.

Rifle Hunting (by Zach Sanders)

**Rifle Terminology 101**

**Reticle** – Pattern of lines in a scope, used to reference a target.

**Dirty Barrel** – Has had a shot fired through it and is copper fouled because it has not been properly cleaned.

**Copper Fouled** – A barrel that is not clean and contains the traces of copper left from firing a round through it.

**Holdover** – Compensation for the effect of gravity as a bullet travels downrange.

**Plinking** – Casual shooting/practice.

**Sling** – A strap, usually made of leather or heavyweight synthetic material, used to carry a rifle.

## Introduction

Probably the best option for the beginning hunter is rifle hunting. It will offer more simplicity and increase the range at which you are capable of harvesting an elk. Rifle hunting will require a few basic tools and a little general knowhow, but before you know it, you'll be ready to take to the woods with a tag in your pocket and a gun in your hands.

If you are about to buy/build a rifle for elk hunting, I encourage you to think of the rifle as a combination of parts. Ultimately, each component is important to the efficient operation of the system as a whole.

## Caliber Selection

The number of caliber varieties out there are daunting, to say the least. When it comes to elk or any big game hunting, there are four things to consider when selecting a rifle for these hunts: performance, price of ammo, comfort, and ammo availability.

## Performance

This is an obvious factor, though it is all too often the only one considered when selecting a caliber for elk hunting. Most states have a legal minimum, a 6mm or a .243. I believe the verbiage used in most regulations is ".24 caliber or larger," so the 6m or .243 are the smallest you are legally allowed to hunt with. The reality is that any caliber deemed legal by the governing authority is sufficient for elk hunting. If you already have a rifle of this caliber and are comfortable shooting it, look no further, but if you don't, there are plenty of options out there.

The two things I compare in an elk cartridge are the foot pounds of energy down range and the trajectory of the round. In the end, you want a bullet that can deliver enough force to successfully harvest an elk at whatever distance you are comfortable shooting from, and you don't want to have to worry about how much holdover you need to compensate for a bullet that drops a lot.

## Price of Ammunition

The price of ammo has been known to sneak up on folks. Hunters find the newest fastest, flattest, hardest-hitting bullet on the market and buy a rifle chambered for it, only to find out that the ammunition is too expensive for practicing. Because practice is an important part of increasing your odds of success, I advise finding a caliber affordable enough for you to shoot at least a box of bullets (twenty rounds) through *after* you have sighted it in and *before* you take it to the field hunting. You should be able to find good factory ammunition for twenty to thirty dollars a box at most sporting goods stores.

## Comfort of Shooting

The bottom line here is that if it is not fun to shoot, you are less likely to shoot, and you will ultimately be less likely to make an accurate shot when it counts. I recently purchased a .375 Ruger for an Alaskan bear hunt; to be honest, that gun isn't a lot of fun to shoot for very long. The ammo is about sixty dollars for a box of bullets, and the gun kicks like a mule. Not only should you be able to afford to practice, but you should also be excited to shoot the gun again; it should not be an experience you dread. For those new to shooting, most rifles used legally for elk hunting may be a bit intimidating. I recommend shooting a .22 long rifle a few times, then an elk rifle, and then the .22. This has worked well for me in the past with people who were getting accustomed to shooting in general.

## Availability of Ammunition

Luckily, I have not had to learn this the hard way. My father explained to me a long time ago that specialty or wildcat rounds are fine, but this can become problematic if you find yourself out of ammo for whatever reason. Many of the places we go to chase elk are not well populated; thus, they offer very few amenities. It is important that you can replace your ammunition locally if the need arises. While hunting, anything can happen, so you can expect the unexpected. You or the airline could lose your ammo, you could run out, or you could forget to pack it. I recommend choosing a caliber that is common enough that it will be readily available anywhere that sells ammunition.

When it comes to choosing a caliber, some of my favorite elk rounds include: 7mm Remington magnum, .300 Winchester magnum, 30-06, .308, and .270.

These can likely be found at any ammunition counter in elk country. They are all well qualified for taking elk, and plinking a little won't break the bank.

If money is not an issue and there was an unlimited supply of available ammunition, I would consider: .300 Remington Ultra magnum, .30-378, .33-378, or .338. These are some of the flattest-shooting, hardest-hitting rounds on the market.

## Action

Although I own a lever-action 30-30 that is hard to beat for hog hunting, I'd take a bolt-action rifle into the woods in pursuit of elk any day of the week. Elk hunting usually finds us camped somewhere without immediate access to a gunsmith, and it is incredibly easy to disassemble and clean a bolt-action rifle. I am personally notorious for accidentally stabbing the muzzle of my rifle in the snow or mud; with a bolt-action rifle, the bolt can be removed, and a cleaning rod or small willow branch can be easily run through the barrel to clear it of any obstructions. Although this is possible with other action styles, it can be a more involved process. A bolt-action rifle generally offers better accuracy compared to semiautomatics in the same price range.

If you decide on something other than a bolt-action, be sure to check the state regulations regarding magazine capacity limitations. There are some fantastic semiautomatic rifles out there that are legal to hunt with, as long as you have the correct magazine.

Remington – Model 770 Bolt-Action

Marlin – Model 336 Lever-Action

Remington – Model 350 Semiautomatic

## Brand Name

Once you've chosen the caliber of bullet, you must select a platform from which it will be delivered. There are so many different manufacturers out there that it can be more difficult than selecting a cone flavor at Cold Stone Creamery. A general rule of thumb to remember is that if something is really cheap, there's a good reason for it. Personally, I'm a fan of Ruger, Remington, Winchester, Howa, Weatherby, and Savage, which has become quite a contender in the last ten years or so.

## Trigger Pull

If your rifle has an adjustable trigger pull and this is something you feel confident manipulating, play with it. If not, you may have to take your rifle to a gunsmith for trigger adjustment. As a general rule of thumb, anything around three pounds will be light enough to allow minimal disturbance to the position of the rifle (maintaining a solid rest) as you squeeze the trigger but stiff enough to reduce the likelihood of firing prematurely. More important than trigger pull is trigger creep, the distance the trigger actually travels as you apply pressure before the firing pin is released. When selecting a rifle, I recommend dry firing. Look for a rifle with a crisp trigger, one that doesn't creep but seems to break or snap back as the firing pin falls. If a trigger has any creep to it, you will notice the trigger moving back prior to the firing pin release, and this only allows more slight movement of the rifle position prior to sending a round down range.

## Barrel Finish

Stainless finish is more impervious to moisture, weather, and general neglect. The only problem is that it shines on a hillside like a spotlight in the dark. My go-to elk rifle is stainless, but I have spray-painted it camo to hide the reflective properties of the durable finish. Many hunters do not think rifles should be painted, but your rifle is a tool, and if painting it makes it more effective, I don't see anything wrong with giving it two or three coats.

Coincidentally, I didn't select my current elk rifle for elk hunting specifically, but it was what I had at the time and has proven effective over the years. Spray-painting it just became a way to make what I had more effective while working within a student's budget.

Blued is more traditional, and although less flashy than stainless, it can and will reflect light at inopportune times. The biggest drawback associated with a blued barrel seems to be the rust factor. Elk hunting often involves getting wet, and a hunter shouldn't have to worry about their rifle rusting.

Matte finish is often the best choice for durability because it doesn't rust easily, nor does it glisten, reflect light, or shine.

## Optics

When it comes to elk hunting, I think it is better to have a scope on your rifle than iron sights. Many times, the closest opportunity you may have at a shot will be between 200 and 300 yards or more.

**Manufacturer** – Not all optics are created equal! It is often said that when it comes to optics, you get what you pay for. For the most part, I agree with this, but as with anything, there are exceptions to the rule. If you have the money and want the best money can buy, consider Swarovski, Leica, and Night Force. Depending on your budget, you might also consider the Leuopold, Vortex, and Nikon scopes in the $400-700 range.

I don't recommend going much lower than the previously mentioned brands or prices, but everyone's motivations and circumstances differ. If you must settle for a bargain or budget scope, try it on the different power settings while looking at an object at least 100 yards away. Ensure that the scope can be focused at the different power settings and still offer a clear, crisp view of the target. Do not just try the maximum and minimum power settings. This is sometimes difficult in a department or specialty store, but if you are interested in buying it, they shouldn't have a problem escorting you outside to play with the toys before you invest in them.

**Power** – I prefer a variable power (adjustable) scope in a 3x9 magnification or somewhere close, perhaps 4x12. Twenty-power scopes and beyond are not necessary to effectively elk hunt, and many times, scopes lose some clarity beyond ten power. The ability to turn a scope down to a lower power (three to four) is a great asset for those times you are walking or sitting in thick cover. There is nothing worse than having an unexpected close encounter with an elk and not being able to find it in the scope. This happened to me when I was younger, hunting deer, and neglected to turn the power of the scope down as I still hunted through a thick oak bottom.

**Reticle** – Of course there are the classic crosshairs that everyone associates with a rifle scope, but there are many options out there, some of which can help in estimating range, help bullet placement at known ranges, and some that do both.

If you choose a ballistic reticle, one that claims to project the proper placement of a bullet at known distances, I recommend shooting at all the distances compensated for in the scope with the ammunition you plan to hunt with. I have a scope with a ballistic reticle on my elk hunting rifle that gives bullet drop estimation out to 1,000 yards, but when shooting factory ammo, it is only accurate out to about 450 yards. From approximately 500 yards and beyond, the rifle and ammunition I shoot perform better than the scope anticipates. Most ballistic reticles are not caliber specific, and very few are ammunition specific.

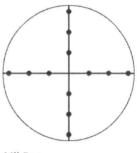

BDC- Bullet Drop Compensation

Mil-Dot

**Rings** – This isn't the time to try and save money on your rifle, because the best scope in the world will be worthless if the rings mounting it to the rifle don't hold it in one place. Many rifles come with scope rings, and some of these are worthwhile, but they must be checked. It's a good idea to apply a little Loctite to the screws of the scope rings in order to persuade them to stay in place.

Vortex – HS Rings

An alternative to scope rings is a rail system. I had used rails in the past for work, but until this past summer, I'd never considered them for hunting. A

guy I spoke to said, "Why have 5 or 6

Vortex – Cantiler Quick Release Rail

different rifles, all with $500-600 scopes? You could put rails on those rifles and buy one really good scope, around $2,000, that will interchange with all the rifles." This is something I'm looking into, though I haven't yet incorporated into my arsenal.

**Level Bubble** –I don't consider a level bubble a necessity; for many years, I successfully harvested elk without one, but I have recently discovered the improved accuracy a bubble can afford. Most people have a tendency to cant the rifle slightly toward them when they shoot, and while this isn't a big issue at closer distances, if the level of cant remains relatively similar, it can be a big problem if you are trying to increase your accuracy at long range while shooting from multiple different positions. If you don't use a bubble, I recommend trying to level the horizontal crosshairs with the horizon with each shot.

Vortex – Level Bubble

### Bipods vs. Shooting Sticks

This is a personal preference. I know people who subscribe to each with undying devotion, but the bottom line is, if you are competent with either, you are going to get the job done. Pound for pound and from a physics perspective, a bipod offers a more stable platform, but has its drawbacks as well.

|  | Pros | Cons |
|---|---|---|
| **Bipod** | ✓ More stability.<br>✓ Always with the rifle.<br>✓ More weight on the rifle is a good thing for helping to reduce recoil, but also to gain stability. | ✓ Added weight to an already heavy rifle.<br>✓ Makes rifle more difficult to maneuver through thick vegetation. |
| **Shooting Sticks** | ✓ Can be used as a walking stick.<br>✓ Usually adjusts faster. | ✓ Less stable.<br>✓ Can be forgotten in camp or in the field. |

## Sighting-In

If the rifle is new and has never been fired, it's important to bore sight the rifle prior to firing the first shot (see "Break-in Procedures"). Several places sell bore sighting lights and doodads, but this can be done yourself by removing the bolt and looking through the barrel at the target. Immobilize your rifle and adjust the scope so the crosshairs are on the target when you can see the target through the barrel. Once the rifle is bore sighted, fire a shot at a large, close target and adjust the scope accordingly. Most scopes are adjusted in quarter-minute of angle (MOA) increments. This means each click of the knob will move the crosshairs approximately a quarter of an inch at 100 yards. If you are shooting at a target twenty-five yard away, it will take four clicks to move the impact of the round a quarter of an inch. When sighting in initially at close range, it is not important to fire groups, one round at a time is fine, but it is important to fire from a steady shooting position. A shooting bench, sandbags, and/or a bipod help to create a steady rest. When the rifle is on target at 25 yards, sight it in at 100 using the same process, only this time, fire 3 shot groups and adjust your scope based on the center of the group.

## Sighting-In Distance

A very common distance for sighting your rifle in is 100 yards. This is adequate and possibly necessary if your scope has a ballistic reticle. If you don't have a ballistic reticle, I recommend sighting your rifle in for 200 yards. This will allow you to make a lung shot on an elk from 0 to 300 yards without adjusting for distance. Most calibers sighted in at 200 yards will be 1.5 to 2 inches high at 100 yards and drop less than 8 to 10 inches at 300 yards. Once you are satisfied with the accuracy of your rifle at whatever distance you choose, it is time to practice.

## Practicing

Many people only shoot their rifles from the shooting bench at the range prior to hunting season, but not many deliver a kill shot during hunting season from a shooting bench. To ensure that you know where your bullet will make impact when the opportunity presents itself for a shot, it is necessary to shoot at multiple different distances and from an array of different shooting positions. If you carry shooting sticks while hunting, why not practice at the range with them? If you like to take kneeling shots, it makes sense to shoot from the kneeling position while you're at the practice range. You might surprise yourself and discover that you are more stable in some positions than you anticipate and less so in others.

## Limitations

We must all have a slice of humble pie now and then. It is crucial that you know what you and your rifle are actually capable of doing in the field. It is important to know what shots you can confidently make and which ones you should keep practicing. I personally try to make every shot from a prone position, using a bipod, because I know this is my most accurate shooting stance in the field, and I am accurate on elk size game out to 500 yards. I have taken elk while kneeling, standing, prone, and sitting. I recommend trying several different shooting positions at different ranges. Being able to shoot accurately in multiple positions will help you harvest elk more efficiently.

**Shooting positions and stability**

- Bone Support
- Muscle Memory
- Close Eyes and Observe
- Breathing

Many people take off-hand shots; sometimes this works, but oftentimes it doesn't. I recommend shooting 3 shots at a paper target at a 100 yards to determine how you might do it if you see an elk. To make your off-hand shots more accurate, use a sling on your rifle and wrap it tightly around your support arm. Tuck the elbow of your support arm into your side and lean your torso back. Keep your feet wide and your legs locked.

Standing

There are a few variations of the kneeling position, and your capabilities for

Kneeling

these will depend on your flexibility. Low kneeling is the most stable and is somewhat of a hybrid kneeling/sitting position.

For traditional kneeling, place your firing side knee on the ground and rest your rear on your heel.

The least stable is high kneeling, in which your firing side knee is on the ground and your support side elbow rests on the up knee.

In all the kneeling positions, the sling wrap of the support arm will help improve stability.

Sitting, Not Crossed

Sitting, Crossed-Legged

There are two versions of the sitting position: crossed-leg and not crossed. In the crossed-leg stance you will cross your legs Indian-style and rest your elbows on or preferably in front of your knees. In the not-crossed style, you will place your feet flat on the ground with your knees up; again, you will either place your elbows on your knees or preferably in front of them.

Prone

My favorite—and, coincidentally, the most stable—shooting position is prone. In prone position, you will lie as flat as possible on the ground. Your legs should be spread, with your toes turned out and your heels making contact with the ground. Your body should be at a comfortable angle while you aim the rifle. It is best to keep as much of your body behind the rifle as possible, and many try to keep their closest leg in line with the rifle, as this will help absorb recoil. Your support hand position will vary with the type of rest you are using. If you are not using a rest, it is best to adjust your sling and wrap your support arm through it to create a firm connection between the rifle to your hand and arm. Your elbow will become the point of contact for the forward part to rest upon. If you are shooting on sandbags or a bipod, I recommend tucking the support hand under the buttstock to add support to the rear of the rifle.

If you are using a bipod, it is best to load it, to apply slight forward, positive pressure on the legs while taking the shot. This will increase the stability of whatever position you are in.

**Ammunition**

As anyone who reloads can tell you, rifles can shoot each variation of ammunition in wildly different ways. I shoot factory ammo because it works, and I have no interest in reloading. The important thing to keep in mind once you select ammunition is to stay with it. If you change ammunition, you should shoot another group to ensure that the new ammunition performs the same as the old with your current zero.

**Break-in Procedures**

The most important thing about breaking a rifle in is cleaning it. There are several different theories about how it ought to be done, but the short version is to clean the chamber and barrel more frequently than you will after the break-in period. Some suggest that you clean your new rifle after every shot for the first 20 shots, then every 5 shots until you've fired 100 rounds through it. I know people who have bought new rifles, shot a box of bullets, and gone hunting without ever cleaning the rifle. This lack of attention to your weapon may diminish the accuracy or life of the barrel, so it's better to clean it a few times during the initial shooting. If you sight your rifle in and practice but clean it before hunting, you are hunting with a clean barrel. A barrel that has been shot and not cleaned is copper fouled, and this directly and undeniably impacts bullet performance. A bullet shot from a clean barrel will, to some degree, perform differently than a bullet fired from a dirty barrel. Some people can't stand the idea of putting a gun away dirty, so they clean the barrel prior to storage, then fire a shot out of the barrel before hunting. Others clean the barrel between each shot when sighting the rifle in and feel they don't have to worry because they are shooting out of a clean barrel all the time. Unfortunately, some consideration must be given to the follow-up shot. While a one-shot, one-kill record is what we hope for every time, reality doesn't let us get away with that forever, and it's occasionally necessary to fire again. I prefer to have my rifle sighted in with a dirty barrel; that way, whether it is my first shot or my fourth, they'll all end up in the same place.

## Cleaning

Taking care of your rifle basically consists of cleaning it, which can be synonymous with changing the oil in your car. Just as you wouldn't drive your car forever without changing the oil, you shouldn't shoot your rifle forever without cleaning it. Much like vehicle maintenance, the topic of rifle maintenance can solicit more opinions than you or I have time to sort through, so follow these general guidelines:

- ✓ Clean your rifle each time you shoot it.
- ✓ Wipe off any mud or blood.
- ✓ If it is going to be stored for a long time, clean it and coat lightly with oil. Remember that too much oil left on the surface of a rifle with a wood stock can seep into the wood and damage the stock over time.
- ✓ Store your rifle in a dry, well-ventilated place to prevent rust.

When it comes to hunting with a rifle, there is much to consider and remember, but some of the most important lessons we can glean from Zach's sage advice are:

- ✓ Always take extra ammo everywhere!
- ✓ If you have one, take a backup.
- ✓ Practice leads to confidence, and confidence leads to a full freezer.

Archery
## Bows

I've been shooting a bow as long as I can remember. I suppose it all started with a toy, a flexible piece of plastic and arrows with suction-cup tips. At that young age, I fell in love with casting an arrow and watching it arch toward its intended target. These days, my bull's-eyes are a bit larger and more mobile than the little paper or plastic ones I used to shoot at, but I love it just the same.

There are two main types of bows, compound and traditional (such as longbows, flatbows, and recurves). Both have their strengths and weaknesses, and I use them both. Most archers today prefer compounds, as they're much easier to learn and are more accurate at greater distances. However, they lack the simplicity of traditional recurves or longbows and have many more mechanical parts that are prone to failure. Traditional archers are also typically able to execute shots more quickly, and this can be very advantageous in a hunting situation. However, becoming proficient with a recurve or longbow requires lots and lots of practice and repetition, and shot distance will be shorter. Traditional tackle requires such dedication that, for many, it becomes a lifestyle. Traditional archers who are consistently successful are, in my opinion, in a class of their own, the true pros of the archery world. Statistically speaking, however, most archers and bowhunters reading this book will be much more likely to shoot a compound bow, so we will focus on that for the remainder of this chapter.

The first step in selecting a bow/arrow setup is being fitted by a qualified pro shop. A competent shop will begin by determining your draw length, which builds the foundation of overall good form. Next, the appropriate draw weight must be determined. Most elk hunting bows will be in the fifty- to seventy-pound range. As with rifle hunting, it is necessary to check the legal requirements for the state in which you intend to hunt. Colorado has a minimum drawn weight of thirty-five pounds for big game, but I personally feel this is very light for elk and would encourage something in the forty-five-pound range at a minimum. Also be sure to check broadhead requirements, as most states have a minimum cutting diameter.

It's important to select a draw weight that is comfortable to you. Many try to shoot bows that are too heavy and end up compromising accuracy as a result. It's better to shoot something comfortable—a bow you can easily pull, hold, and aim—than to strain. The next step is to find a bow that fits/shoots the best for you. Do not go into an archery shop with any preconceived notions about what brand you want to shoot, be it something a friend or neighbor suggested or the manufacturer that had the biggest ad in the hunting magazine. What fits me well and feels good in my hands may not be the best fit for you. This is where going to a pro shop or sporting goods store with multiple brands and models for you to try can be very helpful.

Bows are getting faster and faster each year, but this is not necessarily an advancement, in my opinion. The faster a bow shoots, the more challenging it will be to tune, the louder it will be, and the more finicky it will be when it comes to actually shooting it. Last I checked, my bow is somewhere in the 300 FPS range, fast by some standards and slow by others. Slower bows are typically quieter and more forgiving to shoot.

### Arrows

Arrows are constructed from a variety of materials, including aluminum, carbon, and composites, just to name a few. You'll also find they come in different tolerances, measured in thousandths of inches. I've shot quite a few brands over the years, and I honestly can't tell much of a difference between the different brands and types. Admittedly, I'm also not the best shot out there; perhaps if I was, I'd have a different opinion about the arrows I'm firing. A good shop will help you get set up with arrows that match your draw length. They'll also help ensure that you are shooting arrows that are correctly spined for your particular bow. Spine refers to the stiffness of the arrow shaft. Shafts have different diameter walls and are built from different materials that make them either more flexible or stiffer. Additionally the length of the shaft will impact the spine of the arrow. Picture how much easier it is to flex a long stick than a short one in the same diameter; arrow spine is a very similar concept. The shaft diameter, wall thickness, tip weight, draw weight, and length will all factor in when it comes to determining the correct spine for you. Easton Archery has a handy online calculator at Easton Archery - http://www.eastonarchery.com/store/shaft_selector/ that will help you determine your correct spine.

I personally prefer heavier arrows, as they maintain more momentum downrange and are quieter coming out of the bow than a light arrow because the mass helps to absorb energy as the string is released. This is something I've taken away from the traditional guys who shoot slow bows (in comparison to compounds) and big, heavy arrows that maintain their momentum after impact. I'm shooting around a 450-grain arrow/tip combo, with a tip weighing 125 grains.

### Release Aid or Fingers?

The choice of a release aid over fingers is a personal one, but most modern archers do use some sort of release aid. These help to ensure consistency with each shot and make shooting a bow more akin to pulling a trigger. The mechanical release eliminates the string torque that is sometimes encountered by fingers shooters as they release, or pluck, the string. Release aids are, however, mechanical devices; as such, they can fail or be lost, which is something the finger shooter never needs to worry about.

### Arrow Rests

I'm a big fan of the newer drop-away rests, as they eliminate any contact with the arrow once the string is released. I hate introducing yet another mechanical part to the equation, but the increased accuracy is worth the risk. You should also plan on spending more money on a quality rest, because this is not an area in which you should sacrifice. Another style of rest worth mentioning are entrapment types, such as Whisker Biscuit. These offer

Ripcord Drop-Away

several practical attributes, the main one being that they won't allow your arrow to fall off the rest before it's fired.

### Sights

This is another component where it is advisable to spend a little more money. While you don't need anything too fancy, bulletproofing is a good feature. Fixed pins are nice, since you typically don't have time in the field to make adjustments prior to taking a shot; things in the real world happen much too quickly, so the simpler, the

Black Gold Widow Maker

better. Look for quality materials like steel or aluminum, the less plastic the better. Any extraneous features tend to get hung up or torn off by an unsuspecting branch, so when it comes to sights, less can truly be more. I currently shoot a Montana Black Gold and have been for some time.

## Broadheads

The best broadhead is a sharp one that goes where you want it to go! I don't quite understand the reason, but there doesn't seem to be any other market segment that is so dedicated to putting out new products at a seemingly nonstop pace. I've shot the same broadheads for years and have no plans to change anytime soon. It's a fixed 3-blade chisel tip, 125-grain Thunderhead. There is no reason for me to switch, and I appreciate the fact that I don't have to make adjustments. Many broadheads have been around for decades, manufactured by quality companies, and these are time-tested tips that produce the desired results. Muzzy and Magnus are two that immediately come to mind.

NAP - *Thunderhead*

It is extremely important to practice with your broadheads prior to heading to the field, as their point of impact is not always the same as target points. While I don't see myself switching to mechanical broadheads anytime soon, they do have some advantages over fixed blades. For one thing, their flight characteristics are very similar to field points. Still, in my world, I adhere to the if-it-ain't-broke-don't-fix-it attitude, and until my Thunderheads fail me, I'll keep shooting them.

## Bow Quiver

You need a safe and reliable way to carry those razor-sharp broadhead tipped arrows in the field, this is where your bow quiver comes in handy. In this area, bigger is definitely better. In a perfect world, we'd only need a single arrow, but as the Boy Scouts so wisely put it, we should always be prepared. The world isn't perfect, and things can and do go wrong in the field—everything from missed shots to shots that don't go exactly as planned and may require a second or third arrow. Particularly with elk, once the animal has been hit, if given the opportunity, I shoot until empty.

I encourage archers to shoot with a full quiver when practicing. Target archers don't like the additional weight that a full quiver puts on the shooting arm, but that's what you'll be holding at full draw when hunting, and it's best to practice under real-world circumstances. It also helps to build those arm and shoulder muscles over the course of the summer as you go about your practice routine.

## Basic Set-up Procedure

Accurately setting up your bow or having a professional do it for you will save you a lot of time and headaches in the long run. A good bow mechanic will have your bow shooting tight groups right off the press. While beginners may not know how to troubleshoot and/or set up a bow, you should be familiar with basic maintenance and tuning techniques, as you may have to improvise in the field someday. There are many resources available that discuss bow mechanics in depth, but judging by the typical shooters at our range, many are taking these steps for granted. Again, the more time you spend getting to know your bow, shooting, and setting it up, the better off you'll be in the woods. For those interested in working on their own equipment, a great resource for all your set-up/tuning needs can be found at Archery Report - http://archeryreport.com/.

The very basic set-up procedure for a bow is as follows:

1.  Mount the rest on the riser.

    a.  Vertically align the rest so the arrow is centered on the Burger button of the bow.

---

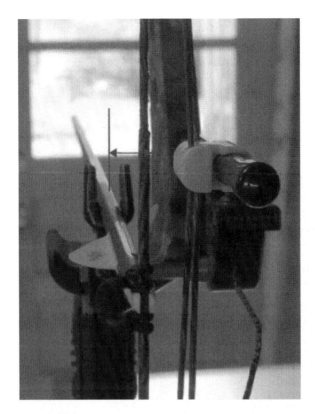

b. Horizontal alignment: If specifications from the manufacturer are available, those should be utilized. In instances where that information is unavailable, the rest should be moved to align the arrow shaft parallel to the riser.

2. Set the nock point. I set mine as a release shooter, so I'm perpendicular to the string from rest.

3. Mount the sight to the bow. Visually adjust to get in the right ballpark.
4. Adjust the location of the peep. This is determined by the individual shooter and should be located to where it naturally aligns with the shooter's eye, without them having to adjust from their natural position.

5. Verify that axle-to-axle length matches specifications and check for any lean on the idler cam. These require a bow press to correct and may be best left to the pros if you're not mechanically inclined.

## Quick Tuning

Here's an easy method to quickly identify that your nocking point (string loop), sight, and rest are all properly aligned. Start by creating a paper target with a heavy black line through the center.

*Nocking Point*

1. Begin with your paper turned so the line is horizontal.
2. Shoot at the horizontal line from ten yards, with your twenty-yard pin, and adjust your sight (vertically) until you're hitting the line. A good rule to remember when adjusting your sight is to always follow the arrow; if you're hitting to the right, move your sight to the right, or if you're hitting low, move your sight down.
3. Next, step back to twenty yards and shoot the exact *same* spot on the target again using the same pin as before. Today's bows are fast enough they should hit the same spot at 10 and 2o yards. If your nocking point is accurate you should hit the exact same spot at this distance. If you're hitting low after several arrows, your string

loop/nocking point needs to be lowered. If you're hitting high, you'll need to adjust your string loop/nocking point up.

4. You can move your string loop up and down by rotating it about the string. After a full rotation, shoot another arrow and verify the height. Continue until you're hitting the line at both ten and twenty yards, as this will ensure that your nocking point is properly aligned.

*Center Shot*

One method to verify if your rest is properly aligned (left to right) is called "walk-back tuning." The goal is to shoot arrows in a straight vertical line as you walk back, shooting at varying distances. If your arrows are not in a straight vertical line and drift to either side, you know your rest is not properly aligned. It's helpful to somewhat align your sight left to right prior to walk-back tuning, but only enough to get you in the ballpark, as the sight will be properly adjusted after you've determined that your rest is properly aligned.

1. Take your target and turn it ninety degrees so the line on the target is vertical.
2. Start at a very close distance to the target (ten yards) and aim for the center of the target with your twenty-yard pin.
   a. Step back ten to fifteen yards and aim for the *same* spot again, with the *same* twenty-yard pin. Your arrow will hit lower than the first.
   b. Step back another ten to fifteen yards and aim for the *same* spot again, with the *same* twenty-yard pin. Your arrow will hit lower than the than the last.
   c. What you're looking for is a vertical line. If your arrows are falling away to the left or right, you know your rest is out of alignment. If the arrow is hitting to the left, move your rest to the right; if you're hitting right, move your rest to the left.
   d. Continue to adjust until all the arrows fall in a straight vertical line.

*Adjust Your Sight*

Now, with your nocking point and rest properly aligned, it's time to dial in your sight.

1. Begin by positioning your target with the line in the vertical position.

2. Start with the target at twenty yards and aim for the center using your twenty-yard pin.
3. If you're hitting left, move the entire sight to the left. If you're hitting right, move your entire sight to the right.
4. Next, check for vertical alignment. If you're hitting high, move your entire sight up. If you're hitting low, move your entire sight down.
5. Once your twenty-yard pin is dialed in, you can adjust your other pins individually by walking back to known distances.

*Broadhead Tuning*

A bow that has been properly set up should be grouping broadheads and field points very closely together.

1. Shoot a group of broadheads at the center of your target, then shoot arrows with field tips. If the two are not grouping together, move your rest, always in the opposite direction your arrows are hitting; if the arrows are hitting to the left, your rest needs to move to the right. Do this in minute increments, until the two groups merge together.

I know many have no interest whatsoever in setting up or maintaining a bow. If this is the case for you, find a qualified pro to set up and properly tune your bow.

I mentioned it earlier, but make sure you've practiced with the broadheads you'll be using in the field prior to heading out; you may be surprised to find they're not hitting where your field points or another brand of broadhead is hitting. I cringe when I see someone opening a new package of broadheads at the trailhead which they haven't even tested. My brother switches over exclusively to broadheads several weeks prior to the season. While you'll be forbidden from taking part in any 3-D shoots with them, you won't have any doubt that you know how your heads are flying!

## Range Estimation

One of the most frequent causes of missed shots is incorrect range estimation. This is something that can be improved upon with practice, but is still challenging under field conditions as rough terrain and steep up/downhill shots, trees and water can skew your perception. This is where shooing in 3-D tournaments and stump shooting can really help improve your yardage estimation. I always keep an extra stump/grouse arrow in my hunting quiver and try to take a shot or two daily when in the field.

While a rangefinder can certainly help in this area, you cannot entirely rely on it. Elk move fast and cover a lot of ground even when they are not in a hurry. Having to operate a rangefinder under such circumstances while still trying to pull off a shot may be next to impossible. A successful shot window opens and closes very quickly; if you're not able to react quickly, you'll come home empty-handed. Whenever you are sitting either for a break or a calling, range several objects so you'll be prepared if and when an animal shows up.

## Using Sight Pins to Determine Trajectory

I wish I would have remembered this old advice on my sheep hunt last fall; if I had, I might have been able to check bighorn off my to-do list, but I made a rookie mistake that I shouldn't have. When you sight down your pins, they'll tell you the trajectory of your arrow at any given place along its flight path. Knowing this can help you shoot through small windows in the timber, verify that you can't get through, or let you lob an arrow over obstacles along its path.

It works like this: Imagine holding your sights on a target that is fifty yards away, but there's a log in your way at thirty yards. By holding your fifty-yard pin on target and looking at where your thirty-yard pin is in relation to the log, you'll be able to determine if you'll clear the obstacle or not. Another example would be if you're shooting through a small opening in the brush approximately ten yards in front of you and your target is out in a meadow thirty yards away. Put your thirty-yard pin on the animal, then check to see where your ten-yard pin is located. If you're ten-yard pin is within your shooting window, you're good to go; however, if your pin is in the brush, you'll need to wait for a better shot.

## Formal vs. Informal

I like to incorporate a couple different types of shooting into my practice regimen, and I call these formal and informal. Formal shots are those fired at the twenty-yard line at the range or a 3-D shoot, focusing on form, release, follow-through, etc. Informal shooting, which can be more fun, consisting of stump shooting, bowfishing, or rolling disks (twelve-inch cardboard circles, glued in six plies, and then rolled in front of the shooters), or anything that takes you out of your comfort zone of a nice, controlled shot. This kind of shooting is invaluable in helping you get comfortable with your bow, and it removes, at least to some extent, the cognitive part of the brain from the equation and forces you to rely more on instinct. The woods are dynamic, and elk will likely not be standing broadside at twenty yards, giving you ample time to draw, anchor, pick a spot, and release. While this is the scenario everyone dreams of, it's more likely to happen like this: You hear branches breaking, something heading your way, and your pulse quickens. Because you're always prepared, you've already got an arrow on the string. You see patches of brown moving through the timber, maybe fur or parts of an antler. As the elk closes the distance, you see an opening or shooting lane coming up. Trying to time it just right, you draw back, and when the elk hits the shooting lane, you have to figure out a lot of stuff almost instantaneously.

What's the range of the animal? Is it the animal you're after, a bull or a cow? If you're hunting in a minimum antler point restriction area, does it have sufficient points? Can you get him/her to stop for the shot? Elk move quickly in the woods, and their walking pace is much closer to our running pace, so opportunities are quick to come and quick to go. If you've put in time at the range, to the point where it all just happens naturally, you'll do just fine, but if you can't answer all these questions almost instantly, you'll likely miss the opportunity or whiff the shot.

# Elk Hunting Gear

As a self-admitted gear queer, I've got a garage full of hunting equipment, including multiples of almost everything. I think the biggest challenge when suggesting gear is that everyone is working with a different budget, and depending on the manufacturer equipment prices can vary greatly. Sleeping bags, for instance, can range from $35 at Walmart to over $500 from Western Mountaineering. For our purposes here, I'll identify the basics and let the reader decide what best fits their budget. Personally, I've come to realize that I'll be elk hunting until I'm old and gray, so I don't mind investing in high-quality gear.

In general, while I do look for quality, I'm very frugal when it comes to spending my hard-earned dollars. When sitting at my favorite outdoor store looking at the racks of hunting pants, one filled with cotton products for under $50 and another with synthetic and technical fabrics starting at $250, I swallow hard while I try to understand why anyone would pay such a premium. After taking that hard swallow and doing my due diligence to find that technical gear at a reduced fee, I now view it in a different light. I still struggle with the high price tag on many pieces of outdoor gear, but I'm willing to spend more in the areas of shelter, sleeping bag, pack, and outer shell (wind and rain) protection. Optics are important, and you should spend as much as you can afford on them, but if you are just trying to fill your freezer and don't necessarily care if you're looking at a 330-class bull or 340, there are some value-priced optics that the working man can afford.

For those penny-pinchers out there, remember to keep an eye out after the hunting seasons wind down, when stores are looking to clear shelves of last year's merchandise. A couple other options are Internet sites such as CamoFire or Steep & Cheap, who offer daily deals at 40 to 60 percent off retail. If you keep a close eye on those sites or sign up for daily alerts, you can get some great deals. If you can handle wearing last year's camo pattern, you can save a ton of money, and I've yet to find an elk who is fashion forward enough to tell the difference!

## Base Camp List

Depending on how you approach your hunts, there are many different options for gear. You may be hunting strictly out of your rig, or maybe you've set up a vast base camp with RVs and tents. Maybe you've got a spike camp back in the woods, or you might be more nomadic, living out of a backpack. There are many possibilities, so this list is intended to be all encompassing. Just determine what's appropriate for your particular situation.

## Shelter

- ✓ Tent
- ✓ Sleeping bag
- ✓ Bivy bag
- ✓ Tarp
- ✓ Sleeping pad (inflatable or closed celled)
- ✓ Cot
- ✓ Pillow

## Weapon

- ✓ Gun
- ✓ Ammunition
- ✓ Bow
- ✓ Arrows
- ✓ Release
- ✓ Miscellaneous tools (Allen wrenches, spare string, d-loop, serving)
- ✓ Portable bow press

## General Camp

- ✓ Tarps or Easy Up shelter
- ✓ Stove (Coleman or Jetboil)
- ✓ Cookware
- ✓ Utensils (fork and spoon)
- ✓ Fuel (propane or isobutane)
- ✓ Lantern
- ✓ Folding table
- ✓ Camp chairs
- ✓ Shovel
- ✓ Saw
- ✓ Insect repellant

## Meat Care

- ✓ Cooler, 200-quart

- ✓ Game Bags
- ✓ Rope or cord, fifty feet

## Food

- ✓ Evening meals (Mountain House, MREs, or precooked)
- ✓ Jerky
- ✓ Granola or Clif bars
- ✓ Dehydrated fruit
- ✓ Candy bars (minis)
- ✓ Tortillas
- ✓ Bagels
- ✓ Tuna packets
- ✓ Peanut butter
- ✓ Bacon
- ✓ Flavorings (onion, jalapeno, spices, etc.)
- ✓ Cooking oil

## Hydration

- ✓ Water containers (5-gallon)
- ✓ Hydration bladder
- ✓ Day use container (Nalgene 32- or 20-ounce)
- ✓ Water filtration (chemical, mechanical, or gravity)
- ✓ Coffee (Folgers Singles or Starbucks Via)
- ✓ Recovery drink (Wilderness Athlete, Gatorade, Emergen-C, Propel)

## Navigation

- ✓ Map
- ✓ Compass
- ✓ GPS

## Optics

- ✓ Binoculars
- ✓ Spotting scope
- ✓ Tripod

## Communication

- ✓ Cell phone
- ✓ Cell phone charger
- ✓ Two-way radio
- ✓ Satellite phone
- ✓ SPOT messenger
- ✓ Extra batteries for all electronics (cell phone, headlamp, GPS, etc.)
- ✓ Solar charger

## Miscellaneous

- ✓ Knives
- ✓ Leatherman
- ✓ Alarm clock
- ✓ Headlamp
- ✓ Flashlight
- ✓ Lighter
- ✓ Rangefinder
- ✓ Bugle tube
- ✓ Diaphragm calls
- ✓ Elk decoys
- ✓ Notepad
- ✓ Pen
- ✓ Hunting License
- ✓ * Duct tape
- ✓ * Surveyor's tape
- ✓ Ibuprofen or other painkiller
- ✓ Camera
- ✓ Video camera
- ✓ SD card
- ✓ Rifle cleaning kit

## Clothing

- ✓ Pants (Sitka Ascent and Mountain)
- ✓ Belt
- ✓ Base layer shirt (Merino wool 190, camo)
- ✓ Base layer pants (Merino wool 190)
- ✓ Insulated jacket (Kuiu)
- ✓ Shell jacket (Sitka 90 percent)
- ✓ Ball cap, beanie, or stocking cap
- ✓ Underwear
- ✓ Gloves
- ✓ Wool socks (Smartwool)
- ✓ Raingear
- ✓ Boots
- ✓ Camp shoes (Crocs, tennis shoes, sandals)
- ✓ Gaiters

## Hygiene

- ✓ Toilet paper
- ✓ Toothbrush and toothpaste
- ✓ Soap
- ✓ Deodorant
- ✓ Wet wipes
- ✓ Lip balm
- ✓ Sunscreen
- ✓ Solar shower
- ✓ Small towel
- ✓ Cotton swabs

## Emergency

- ✓ Possibles Bag (See Bivy Gear list)

## Miscellaneous Gear Tips

**Lithium Batteries** – When it comes to batteries, lithium are better for several reasons that make them worth their extra cost. They last substantially longer than their alkaline counterparts. They're also lighter, do not lose their charge while sitting on a shelf or in your backpack, and they're performance is not degraded by lower temperatures. For all of these reasons, I use lithium batteries in all of my hunting electronics.

**Dummy Cords** – For critical items that are prone to getting lost, a short piece of rope can be tied to your belt at one end and to the items at the other end to keep things secure. This is very wise for your GPS or rangefinder.

**Sleeping Bag Storage** – You should never leave any sleeping bag, particularly a down one, in a compression sack any longer than need be. Over time, the insulation will break down, and the bag will not perform as well. When not in use, keep your bags hanging in a closet.

**Tape** – I've learned from the backpacking crowd that instead of packing an entire roll of duct tape, electrical tape, or surveyor's tape in your pack, you can cut down the bulk by pulling off what you think you'll need and wrapping it around a Nalgene bottle or other such object. This will save both room and weight in your pack.

## Backpacking Gear

Aron Snyder is a backcountry regular and hunting gear aficionado who spends more time in a wilderness setting than anyone I know and loves testing and punishing gear. Any item that has won his seal of approval certainly has mine. In his article, "Backpacking Gear on a Budget," in a recent edition of *Extreme Elk* magazine, immediately caught my attention. The manufactures of the gear on his list are solid, and while some of these models may be updated or replaced, I am confident the manufacturers will continue to supply the outdoor market with quality gear for years to come.

Aron's article focused on backpacking, where weight is always a major consideration. This is not Aron's typical gear list, for as someone who lives and breathes backcounty hunting, he normally recommends different items from the economy choices in the article. If you're interested in finding out more about what he typically carries on his back, I'd recommend checking out his website, Rokslide - http://www.rokslide.com/, which focuses on hardcore backcountry hunts. However, for those just getting their feet wet in a backcounty environment, the list from *Extreme Elk* is a great starting point.

Please bear in mind that the prices listed are the manufacturer's suggested retail price (MSRP) at the time of article printing (Spring, 2013), and prices and availability are subject to change:

- ✓ Shelter – REI Quarter Dome T1 - 3lbs 7oz - $219
- ✓ Sleeping pad- Thermarest Ridgerest - 14oz - $29
- ✓ Sleeping Bag – REI Radient - 2lbs 8oz - $219
- ✓ Backpack - REI Mars 80 – 5lbs 12 oz - $199
- ✓ Boots – Salomon Quest 40 - 2lbs 13 oz - $230
- ✓ GPS – Garmin Etrex 30 - 5 oz - $219
- ✓ Binoculars – Vortex Diamondbacks - 1lb 8oz - $279
- ✓ Spotting Scope - Vortex Nomad - 2lbs 1oz - $379
- ✓ Bow – Hoyt Charger - 3lbs 12oz - $499
- ✓ Knife – Havalon Torch - 2.2oz - $59
- ✓ Stove – Snow Peak Gigapower – 3.25oz - $39
- ✓ Headlamp – Petzl E+Lite - 1oz - $29
- ✓ Tripod - Slik Sprint Mini II - lb 12 oz - $76
- ✓ Rifle – Savage Weather Warrior – 7lbs - $599

For someone starting from scratch, based on Aron's suggestions, approximately $2,524 worth of gear is a good estimation. Hopefully, you have a few of these items lying around and don't need to build your gear supply from the ground up. To make things easier on your wallet, purchase an item or two a season, including in off-season months when sales are prevalent, until you've built up a collection.

Clothing

As with most other gear, the possibilities are endless when it comes to hunting apparel. Before I dive into the latest and greatest choices out there, I'd like to remind readers that many big game animals are killed each year by hunters in old flannel shirts, carrying an iron-sight 30-30.

That said, gear and clothing that performs better will keep you more comfortable. The more comfortable you are, the longer you'll stay out, and the longer you stay out the better your chances of filling your freezer. Whether it's shedding a few pounds off your pack weight or wearing pants that don't bind with each step, the little things can and will add up over the course of a hunt.

## Technical Clothing

We've recently entered a new era where high-tech clothing can set you back a paycheck or two. Whether or not it is worth it is for you to decide.

I should mention that if you're standing in your favorite sporting goods store looking at the high-tech clothing, wondering how much trouble you'll be in with the wife if you spend $300 on a pair of pants, trying to justify the purchase by thinking how much warmer they'll keep you on the mountain, you may want to rethink your decision. If you are only looking for something to keep you warm and you have no trouble huddling over a campfire, you'll likely get much more value from a Walmart jacket than a technical one. The same holds true if you're just trying to stay dry; a regular rubber poncho will do a better job than the fanciest Gore-Tex shell. However, if you want to be able to hike up a mountainside without being completely drenched in sweat in your rubber poncho, going the high-tech route is something you may want to consider.

Synthetics consist of a blend of materials including polyester, Lycra spandex, wool, etc. There are several advantages to using synthetic materials over non-synthetics. For one, they combine qualities from several sources, accentuating each material's strength and downplaying its weaknesses. For instance, polyester provides a great base layer, as it wicks moisture away from the skin, but it lacks durability and stretch unless it is blended with other materials such as Lycra.

While all that is very technical, the thing that most impressed me when I first bought some Sitka pants was the stretchiness of the material. I'd never paid any attention to how much regular pants bind up until I wore a pair that made me feel like I wasn't wearing any at all. It's hard to quantify, but traversing mountains requires your legs to do a ton of work. If spending a few extra dollars minimizes the pain and wear and tear of that extra work on my legs and leaves me less fatigued at the end of the day, I'm all for it.

Try this little experiment: Lift your leg and bend your knee at a ninety-degree angle, as if you're stepping over a downed log. Pay special attention to how much your pants bind up against your upper thigh. As you continue this movement, the restriction becomes even more pronounced. This motion happens all the time in the woods as you make your way over obstacles, and it can take a toll over a day or a week-long hunt.

### Layering

The basic tenant of layering is that you can put layers on or take them off as conditions mandate. Mountain weather typically begins with freezing temperatures in the early hours and can climb well into the eighties by day. These significant mood swings of Mother Nature's, coupled with varying degrees of physical activity, require that layers come and go continually during a day's hunt. One of the worst things you can do is allow yourself to get soaked in sweat, then settle down to wait on a game trail while shivering. In fact, on late season hunts this is often how hypothermia starts. Proper layering consists of base (long underwear), insulation, and shell.

**Base** – Your base layer wicks moisture away from the body. It is said that cotton kills, because cotton that becomes wet loses all insulating properties. Good base layers of Merino wool, polypropylene, or polyester will help move that moisture away from the skin and reduce the evaporative cooling effect it can have. One thing to keep in mind is that base layers made of synthetics will wick well, but they do trap odors. After a couple days in polyester, I almost gag if I get a whiff of myself, and I'm sure the elk can smell my stench too!

I've been hugely impressed with the newer blends of Merino wool on the market, so much so that I won't be wearing anything else anytime soon, if for no other reason than they don't hold odor like the synthetics. I especially like my new base layers by Core 4 Element. I like the feel, wicking ability, warmth, and, most importantly, a camo pattern, which is a huge plus for the hunter in the early seasons who may end up shedding down to his base layers during the heat of the day.

**Insulation** – After your base layer, you'll want to choose a good insulating layer. This acts just like the insulation in your home, creating a space where air can be trapped to keep your body heat in. Good insulating layers will have a high loft; my favorites are down, Primaloft, fleece, or wool. Down and Primaloft are both very lightweight and compress down to nothing in my pack. I'd probably grab the Primaloft jacket if any rain is in the forecast, as down loses its insulating properties when wet, and synthetics do not. Obviously one can add additional insulating layers, depending on the weather

**Shell** – Your final layer will be your shell, intended to keep the rain and wind off of you while letting perspiration out. New materials are coming out all the time that achieve this basic function. As a bowhunter, I have to be very careful that my clothing does not make too much noise as I move about, so I hope manufacturers will continue to make improvements in this area. Currently Cabela's MT050 is the quietest of the shells I know of. Other manufactures like Sitka offer products that I wouldn't consider a true shell in the traditional sense, like their 90 percent jacket; as the name implies, it works well in 90 percent of field conditions, but while it will shed water, it is not considered entirely waterproof.

## Boots

I can't overstate the importance of good, well-broken-in boots. You'll be spending a large portion of your day on your feet, and if your footwear isn't up to the task, it's going to be a tough hunt!

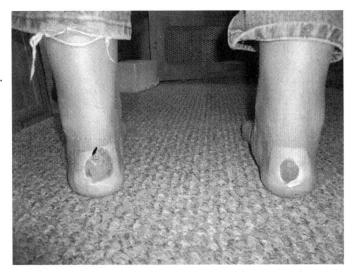

Before you try to decide which pair is appropriate, you need to ask yourself if the feet you intend to put in those boots are trail ready themselves. Don't expect your soft, supple, desk-job feet to be equipped to march around the mountains all day without experiencing some discomfort and agitation. My brother, who makes his living as a landscape contractor, spends a good portion of each day on his feet, wearing everyday work boots. Come September, he never has any problems with his feet, but the rest of us mere mortals must condition our feet for the hunt, just as we condition the rest of our bodies and our minds. If you've been doing so during the summer, you'll have a mean batch of calluses to prove it; if you haven't, you are liable to have a blistering experience in the backcountry.

Many hunters make the mistake of buying a new pair of boots every year, expecting to break them in during the summer, only to never get around to it because sandals and sneakers are more comfortable. Make sure your boots are actually broken in, or they might break you down!

Footwear choices are as endless as everything else in elk hunting gear, and there are determinations you will need to make before you head into the field. The most basic consideration is the time of year. Archery season is typically warmer, so you may not need insulated boots. Late-season rifle hunts, however, might drag you through deep drifts of snow, requiring the use of a pack-type boot.

The second question you must ask yourself is how you're going to be using your footwear. If you hunt from the truck each day with minimal weight in your daypack, you may be able to hunt in trail-style running shoes; however, if you're planning on hauling any kind of weight for any period of time, you should consider a more traditional hiking boot with ankle support and a stiffened footbed. Your feet will be screaming if you load up a heavy pack and take off down the trail in a pair of sneakers; by the end of your hike, you'll likely be feeling each pebble in the trail, and you'll be anxiously counting the steps toward your destination.

Making sure your boots fit properly can be a challenge, especially if you intend to order them from a catalog or the Internet. It took me a long time to realize that I've got really wide feet, so I compensated by buying larger sizes when I really needed wider. I also came to realize that my feet tend to swell a fair amount when they're working hard at altitude, so I have to compensate for that about half a size or so. If the boots are too tight when I try them on at the store, they certainly aren't going to be forgiving in the middle of a high-altitude elk hunt.

Some high-quality boot manufacturers are:

| | | |
|---|---|---|
| Merrell | Salomon | Meindl |
| Asolo | Kenetrek | Cabela's |
| Danner | Lowa | LaCrosse |

Many guys also swear by insoles produced by Lathrop and Sons, Superfeet, Spenco, and New Balance, to name a few, as well as custom orthotics. I've tried a few, but they never seemed to feel right to me, and I don't personally deem them necessary, as long as my footwear fits properly otherwise. However, insoles may be something worth checking out if you're still having issues with foot comfort or injury.

**Socks**

It is highly advisable that you invest in some decent hiking/mountaineering socks. Manufacturers like Smartwool or Thorlo come to mind, although there are many others out there. Most will be made from a combination of Merino wool, nylon, and/or Lycra spandex. The newer blends will help keep your feet dry and comfortable. Also, be sure to base the thickness of your socks on your intended activity. Thinner socks are fine for light hiking, but you should choose thicker ones if you're hauling a heavy pack, as thicker socks will help with cushioning and aid in the wicking process.

**Blister Prevention**

If you purchased boots that fit properly, break them in, condition your feet, and wear quality socks, you shouldn't have much of an issue with blisters. If you do not heed these warnings, however, you may be in for a lot of pain and torment. I'm a big believer in moleskin or duct tape in a pinch, but for either of them to work, you will have to stop and put them on each and every time you feel a hot spot developing. If you ignore slight discomfort, you'll be dealing with a blister problem before long. It won't be the end of the world, but you certainly don't want to blister up on your first day of a seven-day hunting trip.

**Gaiters**

For late season hunts, when there is snow on the ground, gaiters can be a huge blessing. Snow packed in your boots all day long makes for a rough hunt in already challenging conditions. Do yourself a favor and get a good pair of gaiters if you anticipate any chance of substantial snow accumulation.

## Packs

Packs come in a variety of shapes, sizes, and styles, from external frame, internal systems, no frame, and newer vented systems that keep the pack off your back to increase airflow. Although internal frames have come a long way and are used extensively today, I still prefer an external frame when it comes to hauling big loads. These, however, are admittedly not well suited for sneaking through the timber. You'll likely be wearing either a daypack for day hunts or an internal frame for multi-day adventures, perhaps even some combination of the above.

Can you ever have too many?

It seems everyone has their own preference when it comes to pack design. Some prefer lots of pockets to organize gear, while others prefer just a pack frame to lash their own dry bags to. I personally don't need a ton of pockets and keep them to a minimum to keep overall pack weight down, then use sil-nylon stuff sacks to organize the contents inside my pack. I like to wear a pack that will allow me to strap a quarter on in the field without hiking all the way back to the truck to grab another pack. A feature I must have in a pack are load lifter straps; I won't even consider a bag without them.

I remember going on hunts wearing a daypack with enough gear/food to stay out all day. These weren't big load by any means, but by about the third day, my shoulders would be screaming at me when I swung it on in the morning. After learning some basics about fit and function, I can now carry a 4,500 bivy pack with fifty-plus pounds all week and my shoulders feel great! The most important thing I learned is that your shoulders should not be carrying the weight at all; the brunt of the load should be transferred to your hips. In essence, imagine your body being sandwiched between the back of the pack and the front of the shoulder straps. If the weight is all on your shoulders, they will feel it. We all have different body types, and some of my buddies prefer to let their shoulders do the work, but you should know how to transfer the load between those two points so when one gets fatigued, you can readjust as necessary.

**Fit**

Much like your boots, it is essential that you choose a pack that fits you. A five-eight hunter should not try to carry a pack designed for a six-four torso anymore than he should try to wear the taller man's pants. The key features in pack fit are torso length and hip belt size. A properly fitting pack will place the load lifters approximately two inches above your shoulders; if they are not above your shoulders, they will not aptly be able to lift the pack at all.

**Adjusting the Fit[1]**

1. Loosen all straps.
2. Hip Belt: Tighten hip belt, which should be centered on your hip bone.
3. Shoulder straps: Lightly snug shoulder straps. Remember, the shoulder straps are meant to hold the pack against your body, not to carry the weight of the pack. There should be approximately one to two inches between the top of your shoulders and where the straps connect into the pack.
4. Load Lifters: These are intended to lift the shoulder straps off your shoulders. On a well-fitted pack, they should connect just above the collarbone on the front of your shoulder. When tightened, they'll lift the straps off your shoulders and extend for their point of connection at an angle of approximately 45 degrees.
5. Sternum Strap: Should be positioned between mid-chest and your lower neck and tightened until the shoulder straps are comfortably pulled in from the shoulder
6. Load Stabilizers: Found toward the bottom of many packs, these pull the pack body into the hip belt to help secure the load.
7. Release some of the tension on the shoulder straps.

In general, you want the pack to be cinched down as tight as possible to your body. If the pack bounces around as you move, not only will you experience unnecessary fatigue, but you'll also increase the likelihood of premature pack failure, as you'll be increasing the amount of stress on all the pack components.

---

[1] http://www.rei.com/expertadvice/articles/backpacks+adjusting+fit.html

Optics

**Binoculars**

I'd be remiss if I didn't include optics. If you aren't careful, you could spend the greater part of your children's inheritance on the best glass. If your budget allows, go for the best; names like Swarovski, Leica, Zeiss come to mind. But for the working man on a budget, dropping two to three grand on new binos may not be in the cards. The good news is, depending on your preferred style of hunting and the terrain you'll be hunting, binoculars may not play an important role.

Most automatically assume hunting out West requires big glass. While that is sometimes the case, it is not a sure thing. In some areas, binoculars are best left behind in the truck, because it is too thick, and the topography does not lend itself to long-distance glassing anyway. In other areas, a good pair of binoculars can be a great asset. The point is, if your binoc budget is an issue, confirm whether or not you will even need them in your chosen hunting area. If you do and cost is a real issue for you, Vortex and Nikon are excellent second-tier choices that are slightly more affordable.

**Spotting Scopes**

I know I'll catch some flak for this one as well, but we seldom use spotting scopes for elk hunting. First, we're not big trophy hunters; if we were, I'd likely have a different opinion. Second, in most of our chosen hunting areas, 8x or 10x binoculars are enough to tell if we want to go investigate any further. And finally, I cannot justify the extra weight. If we were hunting different terrain and were more interested in big antlers, I'd likely feel differently and would have some recommendations on spotting scopes.

**Tripods**

In instances where a spotting scope would be beneficial, you would obviously incorporate a tripod in your glassing regimen. And even though I seldom use a spotting scope, when conditions call for long-range glassing, I do like to strap a pair of 10x or 12x binoculars onto a solid tripod. The eye relief of looking through two eyecups vs. one is all the excuse I need on this one, and I can sit comfortably for hours picking the backcountry apart that way.

Sleeping Bags

In this area, a little extra expense is completely justified. In certain situations, your life might truly depend on your sleeping bag keeping your body warm. At a minimum, having the right bag will ensure that you get a good night's sleep, essential for any hunter to keep his wits and his body operating properly. Your bag can also be used outside hunting trips, be it on family vacations, scouting trips, camping trips, so you'll get plenty of good use out of it whether you're chasing elk or just chasing your kids around.

**Down vs. Synthetic Bags** – Down bags are great if you plan on doing any backpacking, as they will keep you the warmest and pack down the tightest compared to a similarly weighted synthetic material. The big downfall of down is that is loses its insulating properties when wet, as I've mentioned before. Thus, if you're planning on a trip someplace where extended rain is a certainty, down is probably not your best choice. Where down does shine is in its weight and compressibility.

I've developed the habit of keeping my sleeping bag in my bivy sack even when I'm camping in a tent. While this may not be necessary, it provides another layer of protection from the elements, specifically because it helps to keep my bag dry and also adds a few degrees to the temperature rating. To take it one step further, I stuff the whole thing in a lightweight sil-nylon waterproof compression sack. I never worry about my bag getting wet anymore, and anyone who has shivered through a cold night in a wet bag understands why keeping your bag dry is so important.

**Temperature Ratings** – It should be noted that there is no Sleeping Bag Rating Institute of America; all temperature ratings on sleeping bags are merely a judgment call by the manufacturer and sometimes a selling point. The big names will all have comparable ratings based on fill weight. If you're shopping for bargain basement bags, all bets are off, because temperature ratings on those labels may very well be nothing more than a selling point, and there are no guarantees.

**Sleeping Bag Cuts** – Your choices are primarily rectangular or mummy-style bags, but several companies are following the hybrid trend and offering bags that incorporate the features of both. I've learned to accept my mummy-style bag while backpacking, but it took me a long time to get comfortable in it, and I'd still opt for a larger rectangular bag if weight wasn't an issue, as I find my mummy bag very confining.

## Shelters

A place to get warm and dry is critical to any good hunt. This can be anything from a RV with all the bells and whistles to something as Spartan as a Gore-Tex bivy bag that only offers to keep the rain off. We all have our own personal comfort levels, so it's really up to each individual to decide. All types of

Big Anges Fly Creek UL2

shelters have their uses, and you'll likely end up with several different types on hand for various types of hunts.

Shelters can be broken down into two main categories: backpacking and base camps. I will focus more on the backpacking options here, considering that base camp gear is typically dumped out of a vehicle and set up. Gear choices for base camps can be much easier because weight is really not a consideration.

**Bivy Sacks** – I love my bivy sack, but they are definitely not for everyone. It's extremely versatile because all I need for a camp spot is a level piece of ground the size of my sleeping bag. The biggest downside to the bivy is that they offer no protection outside of your sleeping bag and are typically used in conjunction with a sil-nylon tarp, at which point you're likely heavier than a lightweight tent. I'll normally show up to the trailhead with both a bivy and a lightweight tent and let the weather forecast decide which one goes in the pack.

**Backpacking Tents** – With any piece of backpacking gear, weight is going to be a primary consideration. Beyond that, there are several things you'll want to consider before shopping for a backpacking shelter. Tents will generally be rated as three- or four-season shelters. Four-season tents are built from heavier material and, as the name implies, are designed for year round use. The Big Anges Fly Creek UL2 (pictured above) weighs in at two pounds and ten ounces and works great for early-season archery hunts. However, I'd be very careful about setting one up if snow is in the forecast; lightweight three-season shelter frames are not designed for heavy snow or wind.

Vestibule size is another important consideration when shopping for a tent. It's very convenient to be able to stuff all your gear in the vestibule to keep it out of the elements if the need arises.

**Floorless Shelters and Tarps** – This is an area which has recently grown in leaps and bounds, and configurations seem to be changing daily. The next shelter I purchase will fall into this category. Companies like Kirafu are making some very impressive shelters. The coverage area is greatly increased while keeping weight to a minimum, without the added material going into a floor and door systems. Used in conjunction with a small, packable wood stove, these shelters are definitely worth a look.

## Vehicle Basics

You'll need a good, reliable vehicle to get you into and, even more importantly, back out of the elk woods. Some hunters own huge four-by-fours that can go almost anywhere, but I am not one of them. Most all of our areas you could take a sedan into, although I wouldn't advise scratching up your wife's Toyota on an elk hunt.

As the weather has the potential to change significantly while you're on an elk hunting trip, it's best to use something other than two-wheel drive, especially if you think snow is a possibility, which is almost always the case in Colorado. I also always make a point to top off fluids before heading out: fuel, oil, water, windshield wiper, antifreeze, etc.

There are also a few basic items I keep in my truck, just in case.

- Jumper cables
- Shovel
- Chainsaw or axe (Given the extent of beetle kill areas across the West, I'd encourage everyone navigating on any Forest Service roads to have a means to clear their path if the need arises.)
- Rope or tow chain
- Snow chains and tensioners (four)
- Water

I've also got quite a bit of random gear stashed away in my truck: rain gear, spare jackets, stocking caps, gloves, etc. This stuff lives in there year-round.

Even if I'm planning on a lightweight bivy trip, I let my truck carry a lot of supplies for me so it will be there if I need it.

## Bivy Gear

Whole books have been written on this subject. If you want to read one, I'd suggest Cameron Hanes's *Backcountry Bowhunting* for a more in depth look at hunting within a wilderness setting. Here, we'll just touch on the basics.

The biggest thing to keep in mind if you're doing the bivy thing is to keep your gear weight to a minimum; this typically equates to more dollars, as the more expensive things tend to come in smaller packages when it comes to hunting gear. You can really cut your gear weight in the areas of sleeping bag, shelter, and backpack but be prepared to spend more to carry less.

Being flexible enough to sleep wherever we end up has had a huge effect on how we hunt and how successful our hunts are. Many would-be hunters are put off by the thought of schlepping a big pack around all day, but it's really not as bad as it sounds. Depending on the duration of your trip, you may be adding only several pounds to your pack weight, and that increased weight can often be offset by packing with a minimalist mentality.

Many hunters fail to realize just how much energy they waste by walking back and forth to camp each morning and night. This year was one of our best seasons to date, at a place we found on a bivy trip several years prior. From day one, we were into elk, but we also noticed that the area where the elk were most concentrated several years ago just wasn't as good. When we saw two hunters sky-lined and later calling in the basin, we immediately knew why our elk encounters were lacking. We also knew the elk were somewhere, and it was up to us to find them. This trip was also a little different for us, as we'd hooked up with an outfitter who had packed our base camp gear seven miles back, allowing us to bring a few more creature comforts, but we also brought our bivy gear just in case the elk were not where we were hoping they'd be.

As it turned out, we found a ton of elk about three miles from where they were the prior year. This time, there were many more elk than we'd seen before. But we made the mistake of hiking down into the area each morning, then hiking back after dark—a mistake we will not repeat. Just having that little bit of extra gear in our base camp fooled us into thinking we needed to hike back every night. We knew better, but we failed to throw on our bivy packs and stay out for a night or two. Without a doubt, I know it would have been a much easier hunt had we done so, as the daily commute was turning my feet into hamburger. So before you rule out the bivy option, you may want to give it shot.

## Five Days' Worth of Bivy Gear

- Ball cap
- Sleeping pad
- Game bags
- Binoculars
- Sil-nylon tarp
- Sleeping bag (in a waterproof compression bag)
- Elk bugle tube
- Diaphragm mouth calls
- Rangefinder
- Knife
- Headlamp
- GPS
- Maps
- Backpack stove and fuel
- Spork
- Mountain House dehydrated meals
- Dry bag/possibles pouch
- MREs
- Food bag
- Socks
- Stocking cap
- Gloves
- T-shirt
- Toilet paper, water bladder, Nalgene container, wet wipes, Chapstick (not pictured)

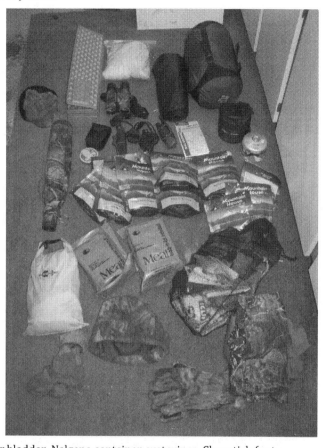

## Possibles Bag

- Dry bag
- Waterproof gloves
- 550 Paracord, 50'
- Water treatment
- Collapsible cap
- GPS Rhino
- Headlamp
- Contractor-grade trash bag
- Compass
- Headlamp
- Flashlight
- Fire-starting kit
- Bug net
- Spork
- Miscellaneous medical
- Hand warmer
- Disposable poncho

This bag pretty much goes with me everywhere I go. It's easy to grab and transfer from my larger 4500 cubic inch backpack into a daypack, etc.

## Fire-Starting Kit

- Trioxane tablet
- Magnesium bar
- Small folding knife
- Bic lighter
- Dryer lint
- Flint/steel

Typically, a Bic lighter (or two) and the Trioxane tablets are all I need to get a fire going under any conditions. I remove the childproof feature on the lighters I carry in my pack, as the last thing I want is to struggle with a lighter with frozen hands.

## Miscellaneous Medical

- Band-Aid
- Moleskin
- Heater from MRE
- Earplugs
- Miniature nail clippers
- Advil
- Antiseptic wipe
- Antihistamine
- Cold tablets
- Superglue
- Buttons
- Dental floss
- Sewing needle
- Cotton balls/cotton swabs
- Duct tape
- Wet wipes

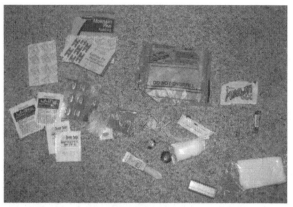

All the above fits into a small Ziploc sandwich bag.

One of the best things you can do for yourself, whether you're just starting out or a seasoned vet, is to get out for an overnighter to run through your gear. I've got a bad habit of cleaning out my pack after elk season and stuffing it with my whitetail/tree stand gear, then rotating contents again in the spring for turkeys. It's inevitable that something will get left behind. A recent scouting trip reminded me of this when my spork didn't make it into the pack. It's a minuscule piece of gear and easy to overlook, but it certainly comes in handy when you want to get your Mountain House food from the bag into your month.

Everyone's list will vary based on personal preferences, but the little things sure make a difference on a tough hunt. Two of my favorites that come to mind and are easily overlooked are wet wipes and Chapstick. Neither of these are deal-breakers, but if you get too much sun and wind, which is easy to do in the high county, your lips might drive you crazy. And after three to four days without showering and no wet wipes, a bad case of monkey butt will send the toughest heading for cover. Giving your gear a test run will reveal these issues before you're miles from the truck; you don't want to grow any seeds of doubt by walking bow-legged with raw, chapped lips. You don't have to go to elk country for a trial run on your gear, as long as you make sure you go far enough from your house and civilization that you're forced to stay out overnight at a minimum. This way, you'll be much more confident when you hit the trail.

Equipment Rental

For those just getting started or someone wanting to do a DIY trip, renting gear may be great alternative to buying and owning a garage full of equipment. One resource I'd recommend is HuntHardcore.com - http://www.westernhuntrentals.com/, as they offer a full line of equipment rentals, as well as hunt planning services.

# Camping Options

Take an autumn drive through the West, and you'll find that your camping options are endless. You'll see everything from jam packed trailheads with thirty-foot RVs, horse trailers, canvas tents, campers, nylon tents, and pack strings hauling camps into the backcountry. There are even the campers who shuttle in every day from

While this camp is about as comfortable as you'll get in a wilderness setting, it takes a huge amount of time and energy to set it up, and once you've started, you've all but committed yourself to a specific spot.

the area hotels and motels, and we mustn't forget the hardcore outdoorsmen who live out of their packs and avoid the roads at all costs.

It's important to be realistic about your party's needs and requirements. Does anyone have a medical condition that requires them to stay close to an accessible road system? Is electricity required for medical devices? These concerns need to be addressed long before heading into the high country.

While we all have our own preferred levels of comfort, a good camp essentially needs to meet three basic requirements: warmth, dryness, and comfort. A good night's rest is paramount when it comes to having a successful hunt, because a tired, fatigued mind and body will ultimately tempt one to sleep in or throw in the towel all together.

Once the basic necessities are met, you should minimize your base camp to only what you think you need. By our very nature, humans are builders and planners; we like the idea of setting up a big, comfortable base camp stocked with food, water, and neatly stacked firewood. Before you know it, you'll be skipping out on the afternoon hunt because the firewood is getting low. Camp will become your project if you're not careful, so make a concerted effort to remember that you're up there to elk hunt, not to build and maintain camp!

Elk are very mobile animals, and this can be quite a departure from the norm for guys who are used to hunting whitetail. When elk feel endangered or pressured, they will hurry to miles away from where they started. Even without pressure, depending on time of year and area, elk may migrate two to three miles daily, and six- to eight-mile loops are typical. Again, we're not talking about elk that live or take refuge on private lands, where talking about public lands with lots of pressure. In my mind the public woods are much like a pinball machine, with the ball being the elk and all the paddles being the hunters.

Certainly the farther you get from the crowds, the more likely elk will be to fall into a routine, and more traditional ambush tactics may tip the scales in your favor. Early season also has the animals in a more predictable routine, a spot we typically hunt for the opener here in Colorado is no more than a half-mile from a major highway, but with the elk still in their summer patterns, tree stands between feeding and bedding areas can be very effective. In fact, those hunts are some of our most successful.

Unfortunately, with the easy access comes lots of hunting pressure, and the difference between opening morning and the following day is hugely noticeable. We've discussed it before and estimate that if a particular section of forest is at 100 percent capacity opening morning, it's 50 percent the following morning and 25 percent the next day. I'm guessing the area levels out around 10 percent of what it was at its peak. For years, we kept returning, hoping to find the elk, without luck. It turned out that the elk were much smarter than us and knew exactly which direction to head for the sanctuary of private property.

The other factor we face, which is an unknown and varies from year to year, is how much preseason scouting occurs. Many guys arrive a week early and start scouting and hanging stands—a whole week! You can guess what this does to our otherwise very productive opening morning spot. But that's public land hunting, and that's why we now never hunt where the elk were and just keep moving until we find them.

**Widow Makers**

Before selecting any campsite, be cognizant of any standing dead timber. With the tremendous amount of beetle kill in the West, this is something that can be a challenge in some areas.

## Base Camps

In my mind, a base camp for elk hunting would be very similar to a camp you'd set up while on a family camping excursion. I should also mention that, for us, base camp usually means tents; if you're towing a trailer or driving an RV, some of this may not apply.

When considering your camping options, remember to build flexibility into your plans. You need to hunt where the elk are. If you're not into elk, you need to pack up a move on until you are. More basic camps are much easier to pack and move. While a big camp with all the amenities can be tempting, they are of little use if the elk are not there.

I will not cover any type of pack-in camps where stock is involved, as it's assumed those are part of guided hunts or that those who already own stock won't be reading this book.

## Spike Camping

While closely related to bivy hunting, when I hear the term "spike camp," I think of hiking to a certain point and setting up a small camp that can be carried in on your back. Typically, this type of camping provides a few more creature comforts than bivy hunting, as hunters typically make several trips to bring in all their gear or even cache food and supplies in the summer to stock camp.

## Bivy Hunting

As I've mentioned, I prefer bivy hunting, primarily because a lot of time and energy can be wasted traveling back and forth between hunting areas and a base camp each day. I know this isn't for everyone, but I would encourage you to try it. It needn't be a weeklong backcountry adventure, maybe setup a comfortable car camp at an accessible trailhead, then spend a day or two exploring from there.

## Drop Camps

While the primary focus of this book is public land DIY hunts, drop camps may be a great solution for some hunters. These allow you to get farther back into areas that may be out of reach on foot. Your basic camp, tent, woodstove, cooking supplies, and firewood will typically be provided for you; most importantly, the outfitter will be able to pack out game. Over the past several seasons, we've utilized the help of a local outfitter to help with our packing, and it's been a wonderful experience. As with any guided hunt, you must do your research and determine if this option is for you. One resource I'd recommend is the outfitter review section on Bowsite, Outfitter Reviews - http://www.bowsite.com/bowsite/OUTFITTERREPORTS/outfitter.cfm

## Forest Service and Bureau of Land Management (BLM)

In the West, we're fortunate to have access to vast expanses of public ground, giving everyone the opportunity to hunt. Laws vary from state to state, so make sure you understand what the rules are in the area where you plan to hunt. In Colorado, it's up to the individual to know where they are at all times. Private property boundaries do not have to be

Expect trailheads to be busy in the fall.

fenced or posted by a landowner, and it is your responsibility to know if you are trespassing.

There are a couple things to keep in mind when hunting on Forest Service grounds. In general, most areas marked on your *Gazetteer* map as Forest Service property will be fairly easy to navigate. You'll likely pull up to a trailhead and have miles and miles to roam without crossing a fence or running into a private property sign, but you must remember that these lands do change hands now and then, and maps are not always up to date. Also, be aware that the Forest Service leases land for various reasons (mining, forestry, recreation, ski resorts, etc.), so it's possible for someone to have mining or logging rights and a private access, so property may be gated. If you get into situations like these, you may second-guess yourself, wondering if you really know where you are and where you're allowed to be. The only way to be 100 percent sure that you aren't trespassing and that you are legally hunting on legal grounds is to contact the county assessor and find out who has the deed to any given property. This would also be a good question to review on your call to the biologist. I would say 90 to 100 percent of the time, it's pretty straightforward, and you'll know with certainty that you are, in fact, hunting public ground. Just be aware of those unique situations that require some additional research and permission requests on your end.

Another good resource to help identify land ownership is Hunting GPS Maps - http://www.huntinggpsmaps.com/. They provide software that displays land ownership on your portable GPS device or home computer. These maps are available via download or an SD card, depending on your particular requirements, and maps can be purchased by state. Technology like this is revolutionizing how people go about gathering data and planning hunts, and it is a good idea to use it.

It's also important to remember that "corner jumping" is illegal. When there are four sections of land, each being 1 mile or 640 acres square, you cannot legally cross the intersection of the four corners if one of them is private property. Technically, the airspace above the deeded property belongs to the landowner as well. Many landowners do not enforce this, but there are definitely some who do; they wholeheartedly understand by not allowing access to public land via a corner they own, they essentially increase their landholding substantially.

**Wilderness Hunting**

In my experience, the wilderness is becoming more and more crowded. When we first started hunting wilderness areas, our basic approach was to scrutinize maps to look for the most remote sections of non-road areas we could find. The trouble was, many guys were doing the same thing, and most had pack stock (horse and mules)—or at least the smart ones did! In more recent years, we've switched our focus to fringe areas; we're not in as deep as possible, but we're farther than many of the day hikers will go.

A quick glance at the map will reveal the farthest spots from any roads, and those areas are where hunters tend to concentrate. But as you expand out in concentric rings from that location, the surface area becomes greater, and hunting density will decrease. This is how we now approach hunting in wilderness areas.

One thing to keep in mind while hunting public land is that you will never be entirely alone. Those trailheads you've checked out over the summer months that seemed all but vacant will likely be bustling with activity once the season opens up. If at all possible, avoid both wilderness areas and trailheads, for masses of hunters converge on those areas.

Those familiar with hunting the wilderness know it's a whole different animal. Your camp is just a speck in the woods, and without daylight to illuminate your path, finding it can be a challenge if you're not prepared. There are no roads in the wilderness to bump into if you go too far (unless you go *way* too far), so until you're comfortable navigating in the backcountry, I encourage a less intimidating setting, mainly national forests or BLM lands.

Navigation is pretty straightforward when conditions are optimal, but with a little inclement weather like snow and fog or a medical emergency, things can get very dicey if you don't know what you're doing.

Finding land to hunt out West is not at issue. The challenge is finding *quality* land that holds elk and not too many hunters. Start planning early, though, and you shouldn't have anything to worry about.

Be Aware of the Weather.

The following is recap of our 2006 hunt, when the weather turned bad in a hurry, putting us in a pretty precarious situation. It all turned out fine, but it could have easily had a very different outcome if even one small thing didn't go our way. Make sure you understand how quickly the weather can change and be prepared for it when it does.

**2006 Elk Hunt**

*Thursday, September 14, 2006, 8:00 p.m.:* Left Fort Collins.

*1:00 a.m.:* Arrived at Miners Park trailhead. Slept in the back of the truck that night.

Mid-September, Colorado High Country

*Friday September 15, 2006, 5:00 a.m.:* Woke up, got dressed, and started up the trail. Because of my unknown schedule this year and the fact that one of the four-wheelers wouldn't start, I had to walk/mountain bike into camp, which is approximately four miles from the trailhead. I was most of the way up the trail when I saw my dad, Big Ron, who was coming down the trail to see if I had arrived. He saved me about a mile, a welcomed reprieve since I was packing sixty-five to seventy pounds of gear. Riding a mountain bike with a big pack on is no easy task and was actually next to impossible, but I still had to try!

*11:00 a.m.:* Arrived in camp. Drew and Big Ron had been there since Monday, and our friend Jeff Blakely had been there since the previous Thursday. Apparently, no one had seen or heard any elk, so the general consensus was that we should spike out farther into the wilderness. Our current base camp was right on the edge of the wilderness boundary, so we were able to use the four-wheelers. Inside the wilderness, no motorized vehicles were allowed, not even mountain bikes, for that matter.

Blakely, Drew, and Big Ron Making Plans

*1:00 p.m.:* We gathered everything up for an overnight pack trip. We planned on packing in that afternoon and hunting the next day, maybe staying a second day if the hunting was good. We split up gear amongst everyone, trying not to pack any redundant items, about forty pounds of gear a piece. We all piled onto the six-wheeler and headed down the trail that paralleled the wilderness boundary, approximately four miles before heading in.

*2:30 p.m.:* Arrived at the trail crossing for Pearl Lakes and Divide trail. It had rained most of the ride up the trail; luckily, we all had rain gear on, so it wasn't bad, but I think we were all having second thoughts about the trip, looking down into the fog-covered bowl into which we were about to descend.

*6:00 p.m.:* Arrived at Pearl Lake after a four-mile hike. It wasn't too bad, until the very end, when it really started to pour. Then we were pelted by an inch or two of hail. It finally slowed down, and we finished the hike into the lake. Luckily the weather cleared long enough for us to pitch our tents and get settled. Everyone was bummed that nobody had brought a fishing pole. That lake was deep in the wilderness, about twelve miles from the truck, and we knew the fishing had to be prime. We started a fire, and everybody tried to dry out, but it started to rain again around eight, and everyone was getting wetter rather than drier, so we all went to bed.

*Saturday, September 16, 2006, 8:00 a.m.:* Woke up to eight to twelve inches of snow and had heard trees snapping all night long. Drew and I got a fire going, because we're both hardy mountain men, while Dad and Blakely slept in. We watched a big tree fall over into the lake while we were getting the fire going. We cooked breakfast of elk steak and chorizo that Drew had packed in. He forgot to pack in any seasonings, plates, or utensils, so we each grabbed a slab and started chowing. The snow was really coming down.

*10:00 a.m.:* We pretty much decided hunting wasn't an option. Everyone was anxious to get back to base camp, where there was plenty of food, beverages, and dry clothes.

*10:01 a.m.:* Decided the hike out was going to suck. By now, the snow had really started to fall, and it was obvious that we had to get moving, or else we wouldn't be able to see the trail out. We all had GPS units but knew it would be much quicker to follow a worn trail than to bushwhack back to camp.

*3:30 p.m.:* Arrived at the six-wheeler after an exhausting hike. We started out at a pretty good clip, but as the trail started to get steeper and steeper and the snow keep falling, our progress disintegrated to a snail's pace. I think we were all pretty pumped when we finally climbed out of the bowl and saw the six-wheeler waiting for us, although it turned out to be a short-lived celebration, because the six-wheeler doesn't do well in two feet of snow. We were approximately 10,000 feet up, and after trying for about a half-hour to get it out, we decided we were going to have to start hoofing it. Unfortunately, we were all tired and knew there was no way we could cover the four miles back to camp before dark.

The "Trusty" Six-Wheeler

*6:00 p.m.:* We only covered about three-quarters of a mile in two whole hours. Exhausted from trudging through two feet of snow while trying our best to stay on the barely visible trail, everyone was ready for bed. We set up camp again, although this time, everything was pretty wet and/or frozen. Too tired to make a fire, we all just wanted to crawl into our sleeping bags. You know you're in for a long night when you have to chip snow and ice off your pants before crawling into a soggy sleeping bag. I wasn't sure how cold it got, but I was guessing between twenty and twenty-five degrees; it felt even chillier since we were soaking wet.

*Sunday, September 17, 2006, 6:30 a.m.:* Drew woke me up and thought we should get moving. I argued that I didn't think we'd be able to see the trail, but I ended up agreeing since the sleeping bags weren't that comfortable to begin with. It's a good thing we woke up when we did, since it took about fifteen minutes to get into our boots, which had frozen solid overnight. Everything was frozen, cold, and wet. We stuffed our soggy sleeping bags into their stuff sacks, hoping we wouldn't have to crawl back into them again. Everyone's legs had been cramping up overnight, so we knew we were in for a long hike.

*8:00 a.m.:* Started hiking the remaining three miles back to camp. We knew we could make it back within the day, but everyone started to question if we could make it to the trucks, which were another four miles. Even if we could make it to the trucks, we didn't know if we'd be able to get them out. Our other dilemma was whether to keep packing all our gear or not. With close to forty pounds in our packs, our backs and shoulders were as tired as our legs.

If we decided to leave anything behind and then didn't make it as far as we hoped, it might turn out to be a really bad decision.

Iceman Drew

*11:00 a.m.:* We had covered a grueling two miles, and Drew and I took turns breaking the trail. With about a mile left before camp, we caught sight of the best thing we'd laid eyes on in two days: Someone had ridden a four-wheeler up the trail. With the snow packed down, we started making up time. Within the hour, we were standing in the last big meadow right outside camp. That was when we were really saved, because the camp right next to ours was still hunting. They had weathered the storm in their base camp and gone out riding during the storm to keep the trails open. We waved them down, and they headed in our direction. We must have looked every bit as bad as we felt, because they asked right away if we needed any help. As luck would have it, they had four four-wheelers in camp and offered to give us a lift off the mountain, which we eagerly accepted.

*12:00 p.m.:* We needed to get our truck keys out of the tents, which were still at the base camp. No one would have recognized it as a camp. Our tents were flattened, the poles broken and the fabric torn. It really didn't look like much of anything. I was grateful we were getting a ride off the mountain and that we didn't have to try to dry out and regroup there one more night. Everything was pretty much left on the mountain: our camp, the six-wheeler, and our trailer in one big, heaping mess. Big Ron was planning to go back Thursday with Jeff and Drew to see if they could get camp packed out. To top it all off, Big Ron's truck broke down on the way back to Denver. I didn't get the call until later that night, but I couldn't believe it, so it was obvious the bad luck didn't originate from my truck!

*Tuesday September 19, 2006:* I sat at the computer, typing this all out. My toes were still tingly, which probably wasn't a good thing, but I wasn't too worried since they still wiggled like they were supposed to. I learned a few lessons from this experience:

1. The cardinal rule for any outdoorsman, which we all violated, is to let somebody back in civilization know where you're going and when you expect to be back.
2. Buy a portable radio and/or check the local weather before embarking on any wilderness adventure. Although the hunters who gave us a ride out said they had forecasted only several inches of snow, it still would have been good to know.
3. Keep an emergency supply box in the truck: extra food, propane burners, stove, shovel, and water. There is likely a more extensive list available on the Internet.
4. Take tire chains and make sure they fit.
5. Invest in a new sleeping bag. Goose down loses its insulation when wet, and it was tough trying to keep it dry out there. Maybe something with a Gore-tex shell would have been a better option.
6. We would normally have had two ATVs, and that may have made the difference.
7. Be in better physical shape. I hadn't anticipated doing any hunting this year because of Beau's arrival, and I used that as an excuse to forego my conditioning. If I had been at the top of my game physically, it might not have been that bad.
8. Don't pack any aluminum cans in your pack. Anything that can leak and soak your spare dry clothes is a bad thing.
9. I think we would have been better off starting a fire the second night and drying out, even though everyone was beat. If we could have gone to bed a little drier, it would have made for a better night's sleep, and we wouldn't have soaked our sleeping bags in case they had been needed another night.

Along with what we could have done better, there were some things we did right:

1. I think we were all dressed appropriately, with rain gear and good hunting clothes. An extra pair of gloves can really come in handy,

especially if your first pair becomes soaked. I was also thankful that I hunted in wool garments, including a wool hat; wool kept me warm even after it got wet.

2.  Drew and I had multiple sources for igniting a fire, and we were able to get one roaring with more than a foot of snow on the ground.

3.  Although we gave Drew a tough time for not bringing seasoning, it was great that we had the elk steaks as a source of protein. We also had breakfast bars, beef jerky, and dehydrated meals, so starvation wasn't a problem.

4.  We all had our own water and a filter, and we managed to keep it thawed.

5.  Because of our map and GPS, in spite of the hidden trail, we always knew where we were and where we were going. That allowed us to make informed decisions.

About a week later, after most the snow had melted, Drew, my dad, and Jeff Blakely went back to retrieve our stuff from the mountain. Our camp was not visible through the snow, and the six-wheeler had snow up to the seat. Drew also mentioned that when we were walking out on the second day and he took

What Was Left of our Tent

a minute to look around, he realized what a bad mood everyone was in. We normally joke around like any other group of guys, but the mood was pretty somber, thanks to fear of the unknown. It wouldn't have been half as bad if everyone had been able to keep his spirits up.

Since that trip, our backcountry skills have come a long way. Today, our packs for a seven-day outing are in the forty- to fifty-pound range, including food. Newer, lighter equipment makes all the difference.

If you enjoy reading and learning from hunting stories, I recommend the following, as these hunters take survival seriously, and you will glean a lot of valuable information from them:

Kifaru – The Possibles Pouch - http://www.kifaru.net/possibls.htm
Kifaru – Emergency List – forum - http://www.kifaru.net/emergency.htm


United States Rescue and Special Operations Group -
http://www.usrsog.org/equip.htm

# Cooking

Heat it and eat it! Personally, I believe the majority of cooking should be done at the house, long before the season begins. I realize that this approach is not for everyone, but cooking big, extravagant meals and having to clean up after them can interrupt an elk hunt and cause you to waste precious time and energy.

Imagine this scenario: You wake up at four a.m. to get back into the basin where you spotted elk the previous day. Things didn't quite come together for the morning hunt, but like a trooper, you've stayed out all day. The evening hunt has come and gone, and you're working your way back toward camp by the light of your headlamp. Since you're elk hunting, you're naturally in great spirits, but it's nine p.m. before you drag yourself back into camp. That great fancy meal you dreamt about back home, maybe a steak over the campfire coals, now sounds like a huge pain in the ass, especially since you know if you get back to the same basin early the next morning, you'll likely have a different outcome.

This is why we do as little cooking as possible while in the field. Our meals typically consist of precooked, canned, or dehydrated meals. If we deviate from that menu at all, it will still be something simple that requires little cleanup, like brats or something similar. Of course we love to devour fresh tenderloins or grouse

Onion- and Jalapeno-stuffed Grouse Cooking on an Alder Branch Rack

when we can, but those are the exceptions rather than the rule, and we generally keep it very simple.

When hunting out of a base camp, we each prepare one or two meals that can be frozen several weeks prior to heading out. These include spaghetti, beef stew, lasagna, burritos, soup, or other meals that can be easily reheated. Another advantage is that we will already have block ice, in the form of frozen meals, for our coolers.

**Midday Snacks** – Several studies suggest that an increase in physical exertion can lead to reduced appetite. Without going into the science behind these hypotheses, I can attest that I seem to have a decreased appetite while in the woods, which seems counterintuitive, considering I'm burning far more calories than I do sitting in the office on a typical day. Something to keep in mind is that you should take food that you actually enjoy. Some of my personal favorites for snacks include:

- ✓ Beef jerky
- ✓ Trail mix
- ✓ Dehydrated fruit
- ✓ Granola/Clif bars
- ✓ Tuna packets
- ✓ Bagels
- ✓ Snack-sized candy bars

- ✓ Ramen mix (ramen noodles in a Ziploc bag with peanut butter, hot sauce, sunflower seeds, crushed nuts, jerky, etc.; the possibilities are endless)

## Coffee Options

Yes, caffeine is a diuretic, but coffee is a vice and a necessity for many hunters. After a couple terrible headaches after skipping my morning coffee because I got too excited about chasing far off bugles, I now keep caffeine tablets in my daypack just for such emergencies. Enjoying a cup of coffee in the woods will help you keep your mind occupied midday, and enjoying that hot, steamy cup can be a calming, comforting way to kill time. I can't count the number of times something has walked past me or bugled in front of me while I was relaxing with a hot cup of coffee. Beyond that, putting something warm in your body on a cold morning is a definite plus. Those are all viable excuses for not kicking the coffee habit for the sake of the hunt. For convenient caffeine consumption during a hunting trip, try these options:

- ✓ Folgers Singles
- ✓ Starbucks VIAs
- ✓ Java Juice pure coffee extract
- ✓ Tea

Another favorite pick-me-up in the backcounty is Wilderness Athlete's - http://wildernessathlete.com/ Energy & Focus powdered drink mix. I don't pretend to understand all the science, vitamins, and other good stuff they put into it, but it does seem to do as they claim and provides energy and focus. Many mix one part Energy & Focus with one part Hydrate & Recover. Our farthest pack-out to date was almost exactly five miles, with a lot of elevation gain and not much trail walking. After hauling our first load of quarters and bivy gear, my brother and I were pretty well spent, but that nice little cocktail helped us catch our second wind, and we hiked back and got the rest of the load and packed it out in a hurry. It was a long day, with fifteen miles of walking, ten of them with us loaded down like pack mules. I'm not saying we couldn't have gotten it done without that Wilderness Athlete boost, but it certainly helped both physically and mentally.

## Backcountry

Our primary nourishment in the backcounty comes in the form of dehydrated meals. Dinner is always a dehydrated meal, and the same usually holds true for breakfast. Mountain House lists their meals as two servings, but most elk hunters will find that they have plenty of room for the whole thing. While I'm partial to the Mountain House brand, there are other options out there. I recommend testing several brands before you head out on a backcountry trip. I personally think they are pretty damn good after a long day in the field, but I don't necessarily have a refined palate.

I've recently started packing Mountain House breakfast options. Sometimes I eat instant oatmeal, but comparing that to my brother's bacon and eggs on one trip made my breakfast seem pretty measly. The Mountain House skillet wrap is hard to beat. It also pays to stock up when companies like REI have annual sales, which saves me 25 percent on my food bill. As for the rest of my meals, they pretty much consist of the midday snacks I mentioned, and I haven't starved to death yet while I've been out trying to fill my freezer with steaks.

## Selecting a Hunting Area

I'm constantly on the lookout for new hunting spots. While there is great value to knowing certain areas intimately, you never know when unforeseen factors may force you to relocate. As they say in real estate, it's all 'bout location, location, location! You might be the best hunter in the world, but if you don't go where the elk are, no one will ever know it.

A good buddy of ours with a great Colorado bull. This bull was taken on public land with a limited draw tag.

Before I even pull out a map or start studying Google Earth, I review success statistics. I'd much rather hunt a spot that has 20 percent hunter success vs. 5 percent. If this means driving a few more hours to hunt a different area of the state, it is still time and gas well spent. You need to be careful when researching hunting areas, paying special attention to why success rates are so high. Factors such as private property can influence stats; an area may boast 50 percent success, but there may be little to no public land on which to hunt. For this reason, due diligence is required.

I recently received a call from a new elk hunter, who'd just moved to Colorado from Nebraska. Even as a seasoned hunter, elk were new to him, and he wasn't sure where to begin. He quickly realized that he basically needed to narrow down the west side of the state. He explained to me that he already had a statewide map with all the Game Management Units (GMUs) marked, and then he methodically went through and determined if they were over-the-counter units or limited draw. Next, he marked success rates for each unit and had a good idea of public vs. private. As he continued to tell me about his research, I considered asking him some questions of my own, and realizing how hard he'd worked to figure it all out definitely made a difference to how I approached the call. It's a lot easier to help someone who is willing to put in the hard work as opposed to a hunter who wants you to do all the work for him. This holds true if you're talking to folks in person, using online forums, or calling the biologist. I'd be willing to bet money that guy had a great elk hunt and became part of those success statistics!

## Online Resources

More and more states and other groups (such as Rocky Mounting Elk Foundation) are beginning to provide Geographic Information System (GIS) data online. Essentially, these are interactive mapping systems that allow the user to overlay data on top of traditional maps. For instance, elk summering areas, calving areas, wintering areas, etc. can be turned on or off. This is an incredibly powerful tool and can greatly help you to narrow down a place to hunt. The challenge to the new hunter is where to begin. Colorado and many of the western elk states are big, with vast portions of public land. These new online tools can help you quickly narrow your search.

I was surprised when I used Colorado's mapping system, Colorado Interactive hunting maps - http://ndis.nrel.colostate.edu/huntingatlas/, and happened to take a look at one of our all-time favorite hunting spots. As it turned out, it was an area where elk's summer range and calving areas overlapped. In this instance, the overlap was exactly where we typically hunt; so while we learned of our spot originally from friends and then boots on the ground, the novice could have just as easily picked the spot from the comfort of his living room in the middle of winter.

## To Draw or Not to Draw: Where to Begin

Although it's fairly obvious and doesn't likely need to be said, less hunting pressure equals more elk. The challenge is that everyone knows this and is looking for that secret sweet spot. There are some things to keep in mind when looking for a place to hunt.

Work smart, not hard! In a nutshell, this should sum up your overall elk hunting strategy. In a perfect world, if I had an unlimited hunting budget, I'd apply for tags in every state out West; because my budget doesn't allow this, as it can add up to several thousand dollars each year just in application fees, I've settled on applying in my home state of Colorado and neighboring Wyoming, assuming that I can still hunt over-the-counter areas each year and can draw a limited area tag every couple years for a better quality hunt.

## Preference Points

Understanding each state's specific requirements does take some time and research and can be a little intimidating at first. For the sake of example, I'll walk you through the basics of Colorado, as I'm most familiar with my home state. Once you understand this, the others will be easier to grasp.

For starters, the state is broken into multiple Game Management Units (GMUs). The GMU map is found in the Big Game Regulations. Many of these units are over the counter, meaning you can walk into any license retailer (Colorado Parks and Wildlife, sporting goods stores, Walmart, etc.) and purchase a license. The remainder of the units are limited entry units and must be applied for in the spring; in 2013, this began on April 2, but the date varies from year to year. I would encourage you to participate in the limited license drawing, even if you're only building points.

So what is this preference point and why is it important? Limited entry units are managed for trophy potential and lower hunter densities. Each limited unit requires a different number of preference points to draw, some being more desirable than others. Some limited units can be drawn every year, and others, at last check, require about twenty preference points, or twenty years of applying before you can draw a license. The popularity of any particular unit dictates how many points are required, as they follow the rules of supply and demand.

I should also mention that some limited units are not much better and possibly less productive than some over-the-counter areas. For instance, west of Fort Collins, there is a group of units (7, 8, 19, and 191, applied for with a single hunt code), limited entry units with some of the lowest success rates in the state. However, because these units are next to a large metropolitan area, the Division of Parks and Wildlife controls hunter numbers by limiting the number of licenses available. I know guys who are regularly successful hunting these units, but they've spent a lot of time getting to know them. So be aware that just because you're applying for a unit doesn't necessarily make it any better than an over-the-counter license.

The good news is if you apply for a license in a limited draw unit in the spring drawing and are unsuccessful, you will receive a preference point, and you can still hunt an over-the-counter area. In the limited entry drawing, hunters with the highest number of points are given preference in the drawing. In other words, the hunter applying for any given unit with the highest number of preference points will be awarded the license. Once you are awarded a limited draw license your points go back down to zero. For the units that require many points, you will not be eligible to draw that license until you've acquired as many points as the other hunters who are applying. These statistics are all online, and applicants can research the requirements for each individual unit.

One important takeaway from this discussion is as follows: In Colorado, even if you enjoy hunting over-the-counter areas, as a resident you may still purchase a preference point for three dollars (currently) during the drawing each spring. If you refer to the Big Game Regulation manual and find the preference point code E-P-999-99-P, this will be entered as your first choice hunt code, and you will receive a preference point for that year. Taking advantage of this will allow you to hunt over-the-counter areas every year while still building preference points. Maybe two, five, ten, or twenty years down the line, you can experience hunting a limited draw unit, where there are typically more animals and less hunters.

A hunter can gain a ton of experience in the right limited area that is managed more for quantity than quality. Talk with the Division of Natural Resources/Game and Fish in the state you're thinking about applying to and find out specifically where this may apply. This could be the equivalent of ten years' worth of hunting experience lumped into a single season, and that's a huge advantage!

**Additional Hunt Planning Resources**

There are several additional resources available to help you better understand the varying drawing requirements across the western states. *Eastman's Hunting* and *Eastman's Bowhunting* journals are great tools for those seeking more in-depth information. Each month Eastman includes a Members Research Section (MRS) that provides readers with an in-depth look into various states and particular units within those states. They also do a good job of alerting readers to changing conditions across the West, including such things as severe winters, droughts, and fires and how these natural disasters have affected herd numbers in localized areas. The magazines contain reader-submitted public land DIY hunt stories, as well as editorial columns with valuable tips for the DIY hunter.

*Hunting Fool* is the next step for those looking for specific information, drawing requirements, and draw odds across the West. They do a great job of gathering and presenting this information to readers. An annual subscription to their magazine and access to their website is substantially more than a regular magazine because it's not just merely a magazine; I think of it more like an encyclopedia or similar reference material. At last check, an annual subscription was about $100. This may seem expensive, but it is really a great value for those looking for valuable, reliable, up-to-date information when planning hunts and drawing quality tags across the West. Their subscription is not elk specific, though, as they additionally focus on mule deer, sheep, and goat.

Finally, those who have more money than time might benefit from hunt planners and tag brokers who can help with submitting applications in multiple states and obtaining tags that are available to purchase on the retail market. Companies like *Hunting Fool* offer License Application Services, and has their own Trophy Application and Guide Service (TAGS) and can help those interested in applying for licenses across the West. As a stubborn DIY guy, I do not personally seek these services, but those who have the resources to pay for them may find them to be of great benefit.

Understanding the varying laws and application requirements across the West can be a daunting task, but when you break it down into digestible pieces, one state at a time, it's really not that difficult. For anyone planning a DIY Western adventure, it's assumed that a certain level of effort will need to be put forth, both in the field and upfront doing the planning. That's what makes it all so rewarding when you finally punch that tag on your public land elk hunt!

## Western States Summary[2]

I've compiled the following information to present a snapshot of tag fees, herd sizes, and hunter success across the West. Please understand that this data is time sensitive and will likely be outdated by the time you read this. However, I do think herd sizes and success rates is valuable information to have and will not change as quickly as license fees. A quick glance will reveal that Colorado has the largest elk herd, but Wyoming hunters are almost twice as successful as Colorado hunters. You may decide where to focus your attention, based on the information presented here and the factors that are most important to you.

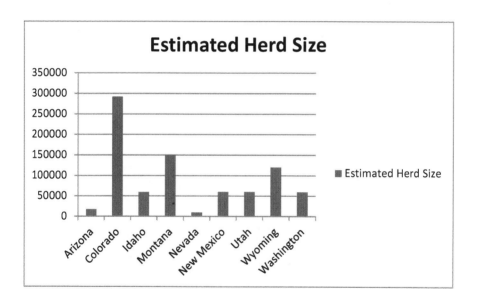

---

[2] http://www.rmef.org/NewsandMedia/NewsReleases/2009/ElkPopulations.htm

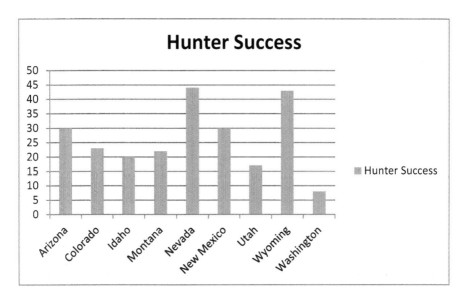

## Hunter Success

Arizona - http://www.azgfd.gov/

- Tag availability: over the counter and limited drawing
- Preference point: yes
- Price: nonresidents, $121 hunting license (nonrefundable to enter drawing) plus $595 elk permit
- Estimated herd size: 17,500
- Overall hunter success: 30 percent

Colorado - http://wildlife.state.co.us/Pages/Home.aspx

- Tag availability: over the counter and limited drawing
- Preference point: yes
- Price: nonresidents, cow – $351, any elk –$586
- Estimated herd size: 292,000
- Overall hunter success: 23 percent
- Remember that hunting with an unlicensed guide or outfitter is a major offense, and this includes paying and/or bartering with someone at the trailhead with horses to pack out your animal!

Idaho - http://fishandgame.idaho.gov/

- Tag availability: over the counter and limited drawing
- Price: nonresidents, license $155, tag $417
- Estimated herd size: 59,000
- Overall hunter success: 20 percent

Montana - http://fwp.mt.gov/

- Price: nonresidents: $809
- Estimated herd size: 150,000
- Overall hunter success: 22 percent

Nevada - http://www.ndow.org/hunt/

- Price: nonresidents, $142 hunting license plus $1,200 tag
- Estimated herd size: 9,500
- Overall hunter success: 44 percent

New Mexico - http://www.wildlife.state.nm.us/

- Price: Nonresidents, $27 nonrefundable fee to enter drawing, plus $562 standard bull tag, $787 quality bull tag
- Estimated herd size: 60,000
- Overall hunter success: 30 percent

Utah - http://www.wildlife.utah.gov/dwr/hunting.html

- Price: nonresidents, $65 hunting license, plus $388 general tag, $795 limited-entry tag, or $1,500
- Estimated herd size: 60,000
- Overall hunter success: 17 percent

Wyoming - http://gf.state.wy.us/web2011/hunting-1000045.aspx

- Preference point: yes
- Price: nonresidents, $577 for permit/$288 for cow-calf permit/$1,057 for special permit
- Estimated herd size: 120,000
- Overall hunter success: 43 percent
- In Wyoming, you cannot hunt wilderness areas without a licensed guide or resident.

Washington - http://wdfw.wa.gov/hunting/

- Price: nonresidents, $432
- Estimated herd size: 59,000
- Overall hunter success: 8 percent

# Scouting

For many hunters who don't live out West, scouting can be something of a fairytale. Those of us who live in close proximity to good elk habitats are fortunate and should consider ourselves lucky. Most scouting starts with some homework at the desk, as a basic hunting area needs to be identified before any further research can be done.

## Internet

The Internet has had a bigger impact on how people plan their hunts than all other areas of research combined. Not only can you pull up a Google map showing roads, streams, trails, contours in terrain, or satellite view, but you can also cross-reference those maps with state Fish and Game/Department of Natural Resource maps. From there, you can instantly hop on an online forum and talk with guys on the other side of the country who can offer advice on local road conditions, weather, etc. It really has changed the speed at which information is gathered and exchanged. Using these tools is a no-brainer when it comes to the first stages in planning any hunt.

Google Maps is a tremendous resource, and for the time being, it is free to anyone with Internet access. Google Earth, another free download, lets you tilt the Earth so you can virtually fly through any area you may be thinking about hunting. Have you ever returned from a hunt and wondered, *I wish I could have gotten a peek over that last ridge*? Well, now you can, with your boots never having hit the ground. I've looked at some of our areas on Google

Earth just to see what was over that next peak or what's beyond the basin to the south. Considering these tools are out there for anyone with the inclination to use them, I'd highly encourage you to take a look if you haven't already. If you've already done so, you already know how valuable a tool it is.

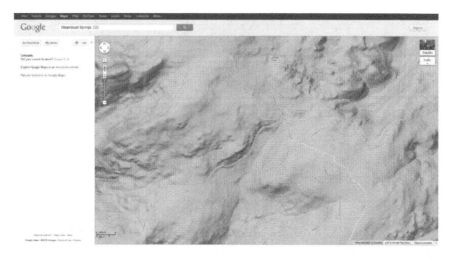

Google Maps, Terrain

Google Maps, Satellite

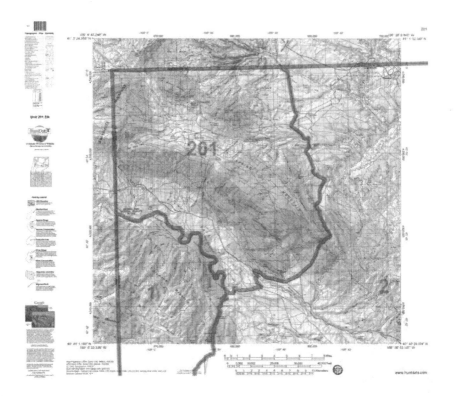

Another great resource is HuntData.com -

http://www.huntdata.com/default.asp. This map shows the GMU boundary, resident herd, summer range, summer concentration, production area (calving), winter range, winter concentration, migration corridors, and migration routes. All they're missing is a big red X to mark the spot! In all seriousness, tools like these are hugely beneficial as you begin to break down the state by varying GMUs and, from there, try to put a game plan together. Unfortunately, at this time, Hunt Data only includes Colorado and Wyoming maps.

In addition to the above maps, though, they offer a wide array of tools to help you plan your hunt, from drawing probabilities, success rates, and kill sites data for hard-to-draw sheep, goat, and moose tags.

**Reading Topographical Maps**

Regardless of where you begin your search, you'll ultimately narrow it down to a specific area. This is when topographical maps (topo) maps will become your best friend. They are frequently called "7.5-minute maps. (In cartography jargon, Earth is divided into 360 degrees. Each degree is further broken into sixty minutes. Thus, a 7.5-minute map covers 7.5 minutes of latitude and longitude). These are the maps I always take with me for any particular area I'm hunting. I'm not sure why, but my preferred spots always seems to end up in the corner/edge of any particular map, which means I must buy multiple maps to cover the area I want to see. Today, there are many online map sources that let you define an area, and they'll send you a consolidated map; this is a great option to save you from having to purchase multiple maps.

While there are many things I look for when reading the map. One thing in particular is steep country, where the contour lines seem to blur together. I can almost guarantee that if the elk are seeing pressure in any particular area, this is where they'll end up, with good reason. Many hunters look at this country and turn it down. While they may be intelligent guys, they will also likely not fill their tags. We go where the elk are, not where we'd like them to be.

I like to concentrate on benches or terraces. Unfortunately, most of the areas we've found to be annual hiding places for bulls won't show up on a map. What will show up is an area that looks like the printers screwed up because the lines on the map run together, forming what almost appears to be a blob on the page. On any steep hillside, there will be benches that won't show on any map. After the season has been going for a significant amount of time, even in areas with only moderate hunting pressure, these are areas we key in on.

**Rubs**

Fresh rubs are always an encouraging find and should be fairly abundant in places with decent elk populations, as elk can be prolific when it comes to creating them.

**Calling the Biologist**

This may be considered general advice because it is so prevalent, but I wanted to touch on this subject because I've mentioned it a few times in the prior chapters. A friend of mine is often on the receiving end of those calls, and he has offered a couple things to keep in mind.

Do your homework before making the call to the biologist. Put yourself in his or her shoes. Biologists are already busy and must now take time out of their hectic schedules to field nonstop calls as hunting season approaches. A biologist may cringe every time the phone rings, but he or she will be more likely to talk to a hunter who has taken the time to look over the maps and create specific questions for which he wants specific answers.

It may be worth making an advanced call to find out which specific maps the biologist/game warden uses (Forest Service, BLM, etc). I know many Colorado biologists prefer Forest Service maps, but it's best to call and speak with the biologist/game warden in the area you're interested in, since communication will be easier, clearer, and quicker if you are looking at the same maps. Ask concise questions in a clear manner so you aren't wasting your time or theirs.

After you've done the preliminary research and are ready to make the call to ask very specific questions, the first step in having a meaningful conversation is to open by painting a picture of the hunt you're planning. Are you using a bow or a gun? How long do you intend to hunt? Are you physically capable of hunting any distance from the road? How far? (Remember to be realistic, for a successful hunt will mean you'll be carrying a seventy-pound sack of meat out on your back.) Being honest and upfront with your expectations will yield more useful information.

Additionally, here are a few other questions you may want to add to your list:

1.  Ask about population estimates from the Fish and Game/Department of Natural Resources website. This will demonstrate that you've taken some research and initiative. It will also help to know how much confidence there is in the model. The local biologist may have a better feel for the overall condition of the herd in their area than what is published on the state website. The information you find online is based on data collected in the field, coupled with population modeling, and the first rule of modeling is that all models are flawed. Many times, human instinct and boots on the ground (given that the biologist has an intimate understanding of local conditions) will yield better results than the models and corresponding information you'll find online.

2.  Ask how the elk population and hunter pressure appear to be trending. A unit's success rates and popularity vary with time, and this information may give you a better idea of what you're getting into.

3.  Are there any seasonal weather variations you need to be aware of that could affect game movement, specifically drought or severe winter conditions? Do your research ahead of time, via the Weather Channel or other means, but this is a good question to ask. It may be

prudent to ask if there's already snow on the ground and if the biologist would recommend Spot A over Spot B. It wouldn't hurt to ask for contingency plans while you're on the phone.

4. Has the biologist personally hunted the area? Be aware that you may want to save this question for the end of the call. If they haven't personally hunted the area, this might create some negativity, as asking the question can seem rude, as if you only want firsthand information from someone more intimate with the unit.

5. Ask how long the biologist has worked in the area. Is he or she getting ready to retire after twenty years, or have they only been there for two months on a college internship? Again, this is one you may want to ask later in the call.

Keep in mind that the biologist may typically refer hunters to the same handful of spots; it's likely you're not the only one getting that information. While it may be a good spot, it may also be a crowded one.

Finally, remember that the biologist may be a hunter and may hunt the area you're calling about. While some may still give you valuable information, others may not be so kind. I've also heard rumor about a guy who closes his eyes and randomly picks spots on a map to tell callers about. Whatever the case, use your best judgment to determine if the information provided is accurate and unbiased.

## Boots on the Ground

My scouting trips aren't a whole lot different from actual hunts, with a few exceptions. If I'm hunting a new area, I spend more time trying to learn the road systems. This is more critical in some areas than others. If roads are minimal, it's probably not worth spending a lot of time driving them, as a good quality map should

Double Duty, Scouting and Strength Building All in One!

tell you all you need to know. If the area has many spur, two-track, or old logging roads, it may be worth investigating. There's nothing worse than packing "way back into a spot," only to find out that the guys camping 100 yards away came in on a four-wheeler. I also rely more heavily on my optics, as I'd rather observe from afar rather than traipsing through prime habitat.

If I'm going to go to all the trouble of scouting a spot, I want to burn a little boot leather as well. I try to stick to designated trails like old logging roads vs. bushwhacking through the woods. Typically, I'm not a big fan of staying on the beaten path, but when it comes to scouting, it still tells me what I need to know, whether or not there is a good concentration of elk in the area. If there are elk in the area, their presence is hard to miss: beaten-down paths, heavily grazed grass, beds evident in the taller grass, droppings, and old rubs. If I can find even a handful of the above, I know I have something to start working with. If you're after a trophy bull, use your optics to locate bachelor groups that tend to congregate during the summer months.

I've been burned in the last couple years for becoming too complacent with a couple of my proven spots, which seem to have gone slowly downhill over the years. The degradation has been so gradual that it's lulled me into thinking it's just an off year, but after reflecting back on it, I realized the paths that were once beaten into the hard dirt now contain no more than a couple random tracks. Even if you are very familiar with an area, don't let it fool you into thinking you know all there is to know.

Scouting is a great time to get the family into the woods. The weather is nice, and the mountains are beautiful. What better way is there to introduce the next generation?

## Hunt Timing: When to Take Your Trip

Once someone gets serious about hunting elk, the question inevitably comes up: "When is the best time to go?" There's no correct and simple answer, as there are too many variables to consider, but I'll highlight a few things to keep in mind.

### Opening Day – Late August/Early September

You have to love opening day. You've waited all year, and the season is finally here, like Christmas morning for big kids! I like the opener for spots where I am almost certain elk will still be in their summer patterns. Hopefully, they haven't been harassed too much by preseason scouting, and you'll get the first crack at them.

Weather can be either a plus or a minus with early-season hunts. In Colorado, it can still be quite warm in the high country on the opener. This can make for nice hunting, but also has its down sides. Warm weather without any precipitation means dry stalking conditions. It also makes meat care that much more difficult. While it will still cool off at night, initial cooling and keeping meat becomes a greater challenge. Bugs can also be an issue in the early season. In some years, the mosquitoes almost carried us away. As I generally don't like to use insect repellants, we wear head nets and mesh gloves. Mosquitoes can be especially brutal if you're sleeping in a bivy sack!

### September

In September, archery season is in full swing in many states. Early September has the bulls establishing their hierarchy for the upcoming rut, and your chances of pulling in that random bull are as good as they'll get.

Mid-September, is somewhat of a pre-rut period, but things start to heat up, and the momentum starts to build as cows begin coming into estrus.

Late September is probably one of my favorite times to be in the woods. If you're lucky, elk will be bugling on their own, making locating them that much easier.

### October

Rifle seasons are getting underway in most states. Early October can still be a great time to hear some bugling bulls, but things will tend to quiet down toward the middle of the month. Cows that were not bred in September come back into estrus, causing chaos on the mountain, which is every rifleman's dream!

## November-December

Depending on your area of the country, winter may start to settle in during these months. Elk won't typically start their annual migration until snow begins to accumulate in the upper elevations. Studies have shown that it takes approximately eighteen inches of snow before elk will begin to migrate downslope. If you're lucky enough to know the location of these annual migration routes and your hunt is timed right, you stand a good chance of putting some meat in the freezer. Personally, I consider this somewhat of a crap shoot; if you're having a mild year or a severe one, the start of the annual migration can vary significantly. Then again, as with most things, as long as you've got your Plan B in place, this can be a very productive time. If you're hunting elk in their wintering grounds, success can be much more predictable.

# How to Find Elk

One of the biggest challenges we faced for years was where to find elk. We did all the prerequisite homework and knew we were in elk country, but more often than not, we saw few or no animals. I'm quite certain we were not alone, as the woods elk call home is big country, and getting into elk is easier said than done.

I've mentioned it previously, but this game-changer begs repeating: Keep looking until you find an elk! A big part of this comes down to mobility. If you don't find any within a couple days into your hunt and you continue to hunt the same spot over and over again, I can make a pretty solid predication about the outcome of your hunt and it doesn't end well.

**Divide and Conquer** – So how does one go about finding elk? While our methods may not work for everyone, we split up and each head a different direction until somebody finds what we're looking for. From there, we'll try to hunt those animals as smartly as possible so we don't bump them into the next county and have to start our search all over again.

If you think you're in a pretty good spot and would wager there are elk somewhere within a 3-mile radius of camp, the real perimeter of that area is 18.8 miles or 28 square miles, and that's a lot of country! To take it a step further, some of Colorado's best units have elk densities around ten per square mile, while other units may only have two per square mile. If you're hunting in a low-density unit, you need to have a pretty good idea where you're going, and even in the statistically better units, you'll likely need to cover some serious ground to find elk.

As we each head in our own direction, we do several things. We look for sign on the ground (droppings and tracks), glass where applicable, and do some selective contact/locate bugling (see "Elk Calling").

**Glassing** – Over the years, you'll gain an appreciation for where you're likely to find elk. It's a great feeling to know you've developed an eye for these places and can say with confidence, "That's a great-looking spot," only to pull out your binoculars and see a couple elk ghosting through the trees. In my experience, these areas are typically edges along the dark timber as it opens up to small meadows and parks. This can be high up on ridges or farther down the mountain, depending on the area where you're hunting.

Mornings and evenings are my favorite times to glass, as more animals will be up and on the move. Once the morning prime time comes to an end, assuming my glassing efforts didn't turn up any elk, I move on and cover some county. I do this as discretely as possible, as finding and then bumping the elk does little good.

## Hunting Bedding Areas

Anyone who has done any hunting is certainly familiar with these areas, though they can be a point of contention for many elk hunters. The general consensus is that bedding areas should be left undisturbed because once elk have been bumped from them, they'll likely not return. Bedding areas are essentially the animal's bedrooms, the place where they feel safe. However, new hunters may not even know what the bedding areas look like. Hunters might spot an area in an open meadow where an elk has bedded down, creating a flat spot in the grass, but it should be noted that is not what we're talking about when discussing bedding areas.

Bedding areas will vary in different terrains, but in general, look for areas of heavy, heavy cover. Within that cover, you'll see where animals have been bedding, if something doesn't go crashing out as you're trying to step over downed timber! You'll also notice an increase in droppings and urine. If you have a hard time sneaking through an area without making a lot of noise, it has all the makings of good bedding habitat. These areas can be adjacent to feeding areas, as they are the places elk retreat to after a night of feeding. You will need to get to know the area well in order to be able to accurately identify where the elk bed down, but with some practice, you'll get the hang of it.

Once you've got a good idea where elk are bedding, should you wait till they go out on their morning or evening travels and hope to intercept them? This is a question you'll need to answer for yourself, as it varies on a case-by-case basis, but I can offer some advice.

Assuming you're on public land, you may be in competition with other hunters. You need to decide for yourself if there are enough guys moving through the woods that someone else will likely bump these elk before you have a chance to capitalize on the situation. It's my experience that counting on elk to be where you left them in a public land situation is a risky assumption at best.

## Night Bugling

If you're still having trouble locating elk, one tactic you may want to employ is night bugling. Even the most call-shy elk seem to let their guard down a little when the sun sets. I use this as a last resort, as I'd rather be sleeping at night than tromping around, hoping to get a bull to bugle. I also feel compelled to point out that if you have any reservations about roaming around in the woods at night, bugling will only exponentially increase any fears you may have. It's been our experience that elk will bugle most frequently on night's illuminated by a full moon, when there is enough light for them to go about their business.

## Mobility

The mobility of bivy hunting, combined with multiple plans of attack, has made a big difference in our success in the field. The following story illustrates how we approach a typical hunt:

**Bivys and Bulls (As Originally Published in *Bowhunter Big Game Special 2012*)**

I stood motionless in the calm, cool morning air, trying to locate the faint chuckles heard just moments earlier. Straining, I peered into the tangle of pines, searching for a tan patch of elk hide. After thirty minutes of painstakingly inching forward, I heard a very familiar cow call, followed shortly by a whistle from my brother Drew. Somehow, we had ended up in the same patch of timber, even though I hadn't seen him since the day before, when we'd split up on a mission to find elk.

Our plan was to call each other on our two-way radios and reconvene if one of us found a promising area. We happened upon each other sooner than expected, so we decided to try the plan again. After a quick morning snack, we agreed on our basic directions for travel and went our separate ways. I wouldn't see Drew again for several more days.

A bivy camp allows you the freedom to move with elk.

After splitting up, I walked down the trail to the east and spent the rest of the day finding fresher and fresher elk sign but nothing that justified calling Drew on the radio. That night, I slept in my bivy sack, and the next morning, I began working my way toward the top of the steep drainage I'd slept in. It wasn't long before I spotted a bull feeding on the opposite slope...

Staying mobile has had a tremendous impact on our overall bowhunting success. For many years, we'd pick a spot to hunt and hunt out of that camp all season. Our typical twenty-mile radius now includes a Plan A, Plan B, etc. If we don't find elk, we move on to the next plan. We've also started carrying our camp on our backs, bivy hunting. I'll be the first to admit that bivy hunting isn't for everyone, but even if you don't bivy hunt, remember to stay flexible in your plans. If you don't find elk, move on to the next spot. The toughest part of public land elk hunting is finding the elk!

I decided to walk parallel with the bull toward the top of the drainage, which terminated into a small shelf where the walls were near vertical, with the exception of a small bench. I thought this looked like a likely place for him to end up, so I eased into an ambush spot and gave a couple soft cow

The Bull I Shadowed up the Drainage

calls.

Moments after calling, I could hear the distinct sounds of antlers against pine branches. I looked up and saw at eighty yards the top of a small tree bending back and forth. Seconds later, the bull headed my way, and as he passed behind the last tree, I came to full draw. At forty yards, I whistled to stop him, and my arrow was gone. He spun at the shot and had run back in the direction he'd come from. I found a clean arrow, though, so I knew I'd missed!

Since we started bivy hunting, most of our nights are spent trying to find a spot flat enough that we won't roll down the side of the mountain. I spent the last hours of the afternoon working toward a large, relatively flat meadow. I got there before dark and enjoyed a good night's sleep on level ground. The next morning, I was walking in the dark, trying to get to a spot that looked good on the map. I'd just topped a large hill and was hoping for a steep, dark drainage, but instead I found a deep aspen bowl. Somewhat disappointed, I looked down and saw a bull 300 yards below. At that point, it was game on!

I descended the hillside and dropped my pack when I hit the bottom. I heard the bull bugle from farther downhill, so I took off sprinting. I ended up seeing eleven elk in all, including three bulls, but I couldn't make it happen. Still, it was a great morning, and I finally felt like I was getting close.

At that point, I was about six miles from the original trailhead and getting closer to another trailhead to the south. I climbed the nearest peak to call Drew on the radio and let him in on the good news. Luckily, we were able to connect, and we finally hooked up around two p.m. It was good to have some company again. We found a couple elk that afternoon, but the swirling wind kept us from chasing them.

We were also able to reach our dad, Big Ron, by cell phone, and we made plans to meeting him the next day. As Drew and I started toward the meeting spot that afternoon, we topped the first ridge and were greeted by a bugling bonanza. At least three different bulls sounded off in the bowl below us, and from the sounds of the bugles, they were having a heated discussion!

We made the amateur decision to drop down after them with the winds still swirling. Twenty minutes into the stalk, our scent drifted down into the bowl, and the place absolutely exploded. We saw at least thirty elk stampede out of the bowl but knew at least three bulls were still down there bugling, not to mention countless cows.

We got smart and spent the rest of the afternoon eating a dehydrated dinner on the rim of the bowl, waiting for the evening thermals to settle in. When the valley floor was covered by shadows, we

When the rain came, we were glad to be close to our spike camp.

dropped back in and made our way toward the bugling bulls. We pushed hard but couldn't get to the elk. We spent the night with bulls bugling within 100 yards of our bivys. Hearing hooves stomping and branches breaking throughout the night, I felt like we were sleeping in the middle of a corral!

The next morning, we followed the herd up out of the basin; amazingly, they went in the direction we needed to go to meet Dad. Drew was able to close to within twenty-five yards of a great bull, but when the bull presented a shot, his vitals were obscured by brush.

After meeting up with Dad, we ate a quick lunch and headed back toward what we'd dubbed "Elk Valley." We set up a small spike camp to call home for the remainder of the trip, then headed out for a quick evening hunt.

The area looked deserted, without many tracks or droppings, but all of a sudden, a bull screamed from fifty yards away. I immediately ran in the opposite direction and screamed back. I threw in some chuckles and cow calls, hoping he'd think I was a bull with cows and maybe present Drew or Dad with a shot. Drew was able to get within forty yards, but there was still too much brush for an ethical shot.

It was a good thing we'd set up our spike camp prior to heading out, because it started to pour as we made our way back. We sprinted the last quarter-mile in the dark, then dived back under the tarps, and it rained throughout the night.

I cherish the time I spend in the mountains with my dad (middle) and brother Drew (right).

The next morning, Drew and I decided to head back to Elk Valley, and we were greeted by bugles as soon as we hit the rim. Dad sat in a wallow we'd found the day before.

We followed bugles that morning, but the elk were really moving. Drew and I split up, each working a different side of the valley. The previous night's rain and a steady wind created good stalking conditions. I'd spent an hour slowly working toward a bull that was staying put. About eighty yards out, I let out a couple quiet cow calls, but nothing happened. Then, about a minute later, the woods erupted. From far up above, I heard elk crashing my way. I assumed someone else had bumped them because I heard trees snapping and hooves pounding long before I saw the first cow break from the trees.

At first they were heading several hundred yards to my left, but as they reached the bottom of the hill, they swung around and started coming my way. At eighty yards, I came to full draw. There were about twenty cows with a herd bull and a satellite bull. The herd bull was horning the satellite the whole way, trying to keep him away from his cows, and it was an awesome sight!

I killed this bull while he was herding his cows.

With the wind on the back of my neck, I knew they were going to catch my scent. They did and changed course in a hurry at about forty yards, heading directly up the steep hill I'd just come down. I let down my draw and sprinted fifty yards up the hillside. Breathing hard, I again came to full draw. While the cows were running at full force, the bull kept working back and forth, trying to herd them. When I saw the bull approaching an opening, I mewed just as he came clear, and my arrow was on its way. He didn't get far.

My brother and I hung the meat in a tree to cool.

We glassed while waiting for the thermals to be right for a stalk.

Drew and I had the bull quartered and hanging in the shade a couple hours later. I wish I could say I called him into my lap or silently sneaked into range, but as the saying goes, I'd rather be lucky than good!

Dad and I had another close encounter later that day. We were walking back from fetching water, neither of us paying too much attention to elk hunting, when I glanced up and saw a bull feeding eighty yards above us. The wind was perfect, and the bull had no idea we were there.

My dad quickly closed the distance to forty yards while I stayed back to call. When Dad was in position, I gave a couple quiet mews, and the bull headed right for us. With almost no cover to work with, Dad got busted coming to full draw at twenty-five yards. In hindsight, he should have just sneaked in for a shot without me ever touching a call.

The next day, dawned crisp and cool, and I once again found myself sitting on the rim of Elk Valley, being treated to a symphony of bugles. By the sounds of things, the rut was in full swing, and tempers were flaring. The herd seemed to be staying in the same location, and the wind was good. I thought for sure Dad and Drew would be able to capitalize, but that wasn't the case. That afternoon, Drew and Dad helped me pack my quarters to the nearest horse trail. After the packing, I went to refill our water supply, and when I got back, I heard Drew calling on the radio: "Tell the packer to bring more horses." Elk number two was down. Drew was able to sneak up on a cow and kill her within a third of a mile of where my meat was hanging. The elk gods must have been watching out for us! Drew quartered his cow solo and packed two quarters that night, arriving back at our spike camp shortly before midnight.

Saturday brought our last five a.m. wakeup call, and I headed back down to help Drew with the last two quarters.

Unfortunately, we weren't able to fill all three tags that season, but regardless, the trip was a huge success. I was extremely lucky to share my fall with my dad and brother on the mountain. Coming back to the trailhead with the horse loaded down with meat and antlers, we were greeted by the usual question: "Where'd you find those elk?"

My brother Drew was next to connect with this cow.

# Elk Calling

Hands down, my favorite way to hunt elk is during the rut, when they are fired up and bugling nonstop. There is absolutely nothing like calling in an 800-pound animal that's looking for a fight! My most memorable calling moment took place when my brother and I made our first wilderness trip. The sun had just set, and the minutes of legal shooting light were quickly fading as we spotted a herd of elk break from the timber and enter the opposite side of the meadow from where we were sitting.

This was before we knew anything about elk calling and vocalizations, but it was one of those rare moments when dumb luck intervened; our challenge bugle was exactly what got the bull so fired up. By the time the bull and his cows had made it to our side of the meadow, it was too dark to shoot, but the bull stood a scant twenty yards in front of me, screaming a challenge at my brother, who was another twenty yards behind me. I remember thinking for a minute that I wanted Drew to quit calling, as I didn't want that big, pissed-off herd bull any more fired up than he already was! Moments like that are why I cherish being in the woods in mid-September.

Even if you don't plan on carrying a call into the field, educating yourself on basic vocalizations can make a big difference in your time spent in the woods. For years, we had no knowledge of what the elk were saying when we heard a bugle or cow call. All we knew was that we were close to elk, and that was good enough. In our excitement, we'd typically bugle back with stereotypical bugle with grunts ("Eeewww! Ugh-ugh-ugh!"), not knowing that we were responding with a challenging response to what was typically a non-challenging locate/contact bugle.

Unfortunately for us, one in every twenty of those encounters would be with a bull that was up from the challenge, and we'd experience an amazing encounter that would have us repeating the challenge bugle, even though we'd only lucked into the right situation. How many times have you'd heard that bull bugle and responded, only to notice his next response seemed to be coming from farther away and the next farther yet? There's a reason for that, and once you have a better understanding of why the animals are saying what they're saying, you'll be able to respond appropriately, and your chances of success will go up exponentially.

Many times, the correct response is to do nothing at all. If a bull is going to continue to disclose his position, why alert him to your presence? I want to emphasize that calling for the sake of calling is not a good thing. This area gets a little tricky, as calling elk is one of my favorite methods and something we have a lot of success with, but I'm terrified of encouraging even a single person to hit the woods, bugle in hand, educating all the elk to the presence of hunters.

While calling can be extremely effective, please take the time to understand the basics. At the back of this book, I've listed some resources that have been a tremendous help to us in understanding the noises we hear in the woods. As with most things, the better your understanding going into a situation, the more you're going to get out of it, making your time spent there that much more exciting and productive. Many times, elk woods are so thick that you won't be able to see the noisemakers; but if you know what those sounds mean, you'll have an idea of what's happening, even when they're out of sight.

As you delve into the world of calling, one piece of advice I can offer is to study and learn from your fellow hunters, both what they're doing right and what they're doing wrong. Many elk have been exposed to calls at some point, so they have a reason to be hesitant and not come stampeding in. You need to paint a picture in their minds that there's not a hunter waiting at the other end of those sounds. Over the years, I've either called in or been in calling contests with other hunters. Nobody wants that, but they're somewhat unavoidable on public land and will happen sooner or later. What I've found is that these encounters are probably just as important for learning as actual encounters with elk, and here's why:

1.  Some particular calls are so distinct that you can always pick them out; in general, these are mechanical calls. Anytime someone introduces one of those calls into a particular scenario, I know immediately it's a manmade sound and pack up and leave. I'm sure any elk that's been around the block recognizes these very distinct sounds and does the same thing.

2.  Multiple callers always sound better than a solo guy. If I get into an encounter and am wondering if it is one person or an elk and I suddenly hear another chirp/mew from eighty yards over, it always makes me reevaluate. Again, I'm sure elk are no different. Obviously, if you don't have any friends to go elk hunting with this tactic won't help you.

3.  Poor calling or too much calling is a dead giveaway. A couple of calls I've heard in the woods sounded more like geese than elk. A good way to check your calling is to record yourself and listen to the playback. Having a basic proficiency with whatever type of call you're using before hitting the woods is key to being confident that you'll actually get the results you're hoping for.

    Remember that elk, in their normal day-to-day lives, do not call back and forth nonstop; the majority of their communication is nonverbal. How often do you come up on a group of elk in the woods who are having a conference call? Hardly ever!

Your goal should be to work on things that differentiate yourself from the crowd, such as:

1.  Use unique sounds. My brother does a lot of yawns, chuckles, and moans, not at all the typical noises other hunters make. Even though I hunt with him, half the time he has me wondering. When I'm looking back to make sure it's really him I have to think the bull is doing the same thing.

2.  Sometimes you don't even need to touch a call to call elk in. If you know the location of the animal you're trying to call, especially bulls, and can sneak in close, start raking a tree, stomping, raking the ground, etc. Many times that bull will come in to investigate, even though you've never actually called him. This is a highly effective tactic because most guys automatically default to calling, which I feel many bulls are skeptical of at some level. Again, doing things other

guys aren't may be just the thing that call-shy bull needs to come in a take a curious peek that will be his last.

## Get Aggressive

We used to sneak everywhere we went in the woods, still-hunting our way through the shadows. While this was good practice, in the big picture, it didn't produce results. When you are calling, you are basically pretending to be an elk, so it doesn't hurt to get into character. Elk are not particularly quiet when they move through the woods, and while they can sneak in silently at times, they can also sound like a freight train.

These days, if we get a bull to respond to a call, we might just run in to close the distance. Knowing when and where that distance is only comes from experience. You must hear a bull's bugle in order to somewhat accurately judge if he's 200, 400, or 800 yards away, but with a little bit of practice, you'll get a feel for it. What I've also come to realize is that when running in, the elk can see pieces and parts of me through the timber and won't be able to tell if I'm elk, deer, coyote, or human, etc. Likewise, remember when you see an elk walking through the woods, you'll likely only

Some light cow calling was just what this bull was looking for.

see bits here and there. If you're trying to cut the distance between yourself and a bugling elk that seems to be moving farther away, you'll never catch up by sneaking through the woods. You need to think like a track star!

### Types of Calls

Go to any sporting goods store, and you'll likely be overwhelmed by the assortment of calls on the shelf. Someone new to the sport may have a hard time knowing where to begin, so I've listed the different types of calls, from easiest to most difficult to master.

## Mechanical Calls

These calls only require that the user presses a button. While they can produce very realistic sounds, they are highly overused, especially in heavily hunted public lands. I try hard not to pick any manufacturer or particular call over another, but we can sidestep a Hoochi Mama at a quarter-mile; almost everyone has one, and it seems everyone uses them. This actually works to our advantage because it's such a distinct sound that we can just slide around the guy doing the calling, as we don't want to interfere with their hunt or waste our time trying to sneak in on other guys. I will say that I do think the Hoochi works well when using multiple cow calls, imitating a small herd communicating, but even in this scenario, the Hoochi Mama still stands out, and not in a good way. That said, I'm sure there are piles and piles of dead elk that wish the Hoochi didn't sound so good.

## Hard-Body External Reed

These calls can produce very realistic sounds and are fairly simple to master. The downside is that they require hand movement to operate and need to be treated gently so the exposed reed doesn't become damaged. Other than that, these are a great way to easily start producing realistic elk sounds, typically cow chirps and mews.

## Diaphragm Calls

I use diaphragm calls almost exclusively, as they're very versatile and keep my hands free. They are, however, the most difficult to master.

If you're interested in learning how to use a diaphragm call, I recommend that you pick up several types, makes, and models. While I feel pretty competent using most diaphragm calls, some particular manufacturers just won't work for me. Because our mouths and palettes are all shaped differently, the call needs to fit well to work as designed, and the smallest variations can make a big difference. I recommend purchasing several, as you will likely have to try a few before you find a good fit.

Mouth diaphragms come in many different configurations, including number of reeds. Single-reed calls are usually easier to use and create a call in a higher pitch. Double- and triple-reed calls and more typically used to produce lower pitches and work better in high-volume applications where more air is being blown over the reed.

## Bulge Tubes

Again, there are many options on the market. Probably the easiest to use is the Carlton Qwik Bugle, which utilizes a manual button to control pressure across the reed. While the sounds produced with this call are somewhat limited, it is very user friendly. Another option is the Primos Terminator with an external latex reed. I think these are fairly easy to master and can produce some very realistic sounds. Finally, a plain bugle tube with a month diaphragm is my favorite as it offers the most flexibility and realism, but also requires the most practice.

## Basic Vocalizations

I've left this section intentionally light for a couple of reasons. First, a book is not the best format to describe vocalizations, so I really recommend that anyone interested in calling refer to the references at the back of the book, as they have made a world of difference in our elk hunting.

## Bull Vocalizations

**Locate/Contact Bugle** – This is the sound that forever changed our success in the fall. Because the woods the elk call home are so vast and dense, finding them can be a challenge. If you're hunting country that allows glassing, it can be a tremendous help; if not, finding them can be tough. What we've learned over the years is that by walking through the woods and using a locate bugle every quarter- to half-mile, we'll often coax a bull into responding, and that gives us something to work with. If we don't get a response, we keep moving until we do.

**Chuckles** – These are used by a bull as he communicates within the herd, typically while he's tending he cows. This is a nonthreatening sound.

**Grunts** – As the name implies, this is a more aggressive or agitated vocalization. Similar to chuckles but lower in pitch and slower in tempo, grunts will often follow a bugle in a confrontational encounter.

**Glunks** – Used as a tending call. These are low-volume calls and sound like someone hitting the open end of a glass bottle. They are reproduced by hunters striking the wide end of their bugle tube. I occasionally add these to our cold-calling, when we're working in heavy timber and anticipate animals to be in the immediate vicinity, just to add a little realism to the set.

## Cow Vocalizations

**Chirp** – Used within the herd to keep in contact.

**Mew** – More typically used as the herd is moving. This is a fairly common sound in the elk woods.

**Lost Mew** – Similar to the mew but pronounced and drawn out. A favorite call of mine in cold-calling and when trying to gather the herd after they've been busted up.

### Seasonal Variations

It's important to understand what elk are doing at various times of the year, as this may dictate how you approach the situation. During the summer, bulls will spend their time in bachelor herds. These herds will start to break up as the rut approaches. Around the beginning of September, the smaller herds will begin to disperse. That is a great time to get a bull to respond to either a locate/contact bugle or cow calling. I expect animals to come in fairly quietly this time of year. As September rolls on, you can expect bulls to be together with cows as they begin to round up their herds.

### Calling Scenarios
### Caller/Shooter

While calling can certainly be utilized by the solo hunter, teaming up to call elk will always be more productive. When working as a team, there are several things you'll want to consider. First, the wind should always be at the forefront of your mind. Forget this, and you'll never get anywhere. You'll only end up educating elk, which nobody wants.

If there is a particular animal you're focusing on, your shooter should be anywhere from thirty to eighty yards in front of the caller. As with everything else in elk hunting, terrain will dictate how you approach each encounter. Remember that the elk will be on the lookout for the "animal" making the noise; your goal is to get a shot before they see you, or make sure there is a spot where the animal will pause to look for the "elk" making all the noise. Think edges! Wherever there's a natural break in the terrain, the animal will likely pause at that point to assess the situation. If your shooter is within range of that likely spot, your odds will go up.

Remember that the shooter's role is to shoot. Don't let them touch a call when they're the designated lead, as this will only give the elk a chance to see the shooter that much sooner.

Try to set the shooter at a slight offset to the animal being called. In my experience, more animals have come directly to the call vs. circling downwind, especially when calling to a specific animal. If your shooter is directly in front of you, the elk will walk directly toward him. It's much better if they're set off to the side some fifteen to twenty yards away, offering the shooter a broadside shot as the animal walks by.

There are times when the animal will circle downwind, especially if you're calling into a crosswind. Unfortunately, this will be somewhat of a guessing game, as many variables will affect how the elk is likely to respond. Knowing how much pressure the elk you're calling has seen is beneficial; elk that have been called before will likely approach more cautiously, trying to circle downwind before committing. Still, even unpressured elk may want to circle downwind, checking the scent of the one doing the calling and wondering if it is the same bull who kicked his butt yesterday. Finally, the general attitude of the elk can affect their approach. Get one in an ornery mood, and he may charge straight in, versus the one you just disturbed from a nap. There is a lot that must be considered when setting up to call, and no matter how much we try to understand and anticipate what the animal will do, in the end, it's a guessing game. We can only do our best to make an educated guess.

**Passive vs. Aggressive**

When you hear that bull bugle, you must quickly assess the situation to determine if the bull is worked up and aggressive or passive, as if he's just been roused from a nap. This will determine how you should prepare for the encounter and approach the situation.

Aggressive encounters are likely everyone's favorite. Perhaps you are just walking along and the bull(s) begin bugling. As you sneak in closer, it's apparent that he's already in a foul mood, perhaps because the satellites just won't leave his cows alone. One word comes to mind if the bull is already worked up and there are satellites you might pull in as well: *Jackpot*!

If possible, try to sneak all the way in for a shot. Remember, calling is just one tool in the toolbox. If you don't think you can sneak all the way in, try to get as close as possible, within at least 100 yards. If you have the cover to work with, the closer the better. If you don't think you can get in close enough for a shot, once you're within his comfort zone, you can do one of two things. Sometimes without even touching a call, you can break some nearby branches to simulate a bull raking. You can also use the branch to rake the ground while loudly stomping your feet. Other times, especially if a bull is answering your calls, cow call your way in. Then, at the last minute, once you are well inside the 100-yard zone, bugle. In my experience, bulls do not like it when another bull sneaks in, and they will come to investigate to see who is trying to intercept their cows.

If you think you've got a passive bull on your hands, one you may have disturbed from his midday slumber or lull, approach the situation a little differently. If hunting with a partner and the bull is responsive, this is a good situation to send the shooters up ahead with the goal of sneaking in for the shot, while the caller sits back to keep the bull talking. Knowing exactly where the bull is located can be a tremendous help to someone trying to sneak into bow range. I'm also more prone to use cow calls in a passive bull situation, as a passive bull may be more easily enticed by a loving encounter than a violent one.

## Breaking Up the Herd

Not that I'd ever do it intentionally, but when things go badly and the herd explodes around you, don't start to cry, even though you may feel like it. Get it together and grab your calls, because this is a perfect scenario to suck some elk into your lap. Elk are herd animals, and if those herds are busted up and scattered everywhere, running every which way over the mountain peak, it's their nature to want to reunite. In these situations, calling can be extremely effective, because elk sounds are just what the lost and disoriented elks want to hear.

For many years, we'd just stand there and cuss that we just blown a day's worth of hunting by scattering elk every which way. Sometimes, depending on the size of the herd, you may not even need to say anything; you can just grab a seat, being mindful of the wind and knowing you're about to encounter some stragglers who are desperately trying to find their friends.

Two particular sounds work well in these situations, as they both represent gathering sounds: the locate/contact bugle and the lost mew. Try to get up just short of where I think the animals may have stopped. If they saw you but did not smell you, it's likely that only one or two of the animals even know why they ran. As they hit the timber, they'll often stop, watching their backs, trying to figure out what all the fuss is about. As long as you don't go stumbling right into them, you have a prime opportunity.

# Tactics

## Spot and Stalk

This is a classic method for hunting elk. Because of their size, elk are fairly easy to pick out with the naked eye or with the aid of 8x or 10x binoculars. As is the case with most woodland creatures, elk are most active early morning and evening (crepuscular, for those who prefer to impress their friends with big words around the campfire), when they move from the safety of the timber into the open parks and meadows. We look for high vantage points that let us glass into several different drainages, always remembering to focus on the edges where the elk like to congregate.

When we were first starting out, we'd get so excited when we spotted elk that we'd want to head straight for them as fast as we could. Over the years, though, I've learned to have a little more patience, taking the time to study what the animals are doing, how many there are, and if they are feeding in any specific direction. Basically, I try to formulate an educated game plan rather than of just bombing in there hoping to get a shot.

Once you've found elk in a stalkable position, you should determine wind direction and consider time of day, how the morning and evening thermals will affect your stalk. If the elk are spotted milling around at last light, they'll likely be in the same vicinity at sunup; make it a priority to be at that location by first light.

When starting a stalk over any great distance, be sure to mentally assess the landscape prior to heading off, as it will likely look much different once you've moved in close to the animals. Look for any unique features that stand out and it may be beneficial to make a quick sketch or snap a photo with a digital camera that you can reference later during the stalk.

Before you begin your stalk, figure out how you'll use the terrain to your advantage to quickly cover ground without having to worry about being seen. In my experience, elk are typically moving at a slower pace in the evening as they filter out from the timber. Elk spotted in the morning seem to be in a hurry to get back into some type of cover. This is a general rule, and there will always be exceptions, but when I spot elk in the morning, I'm always far more anxious to close in more quickly than when I spot them in the evening.

Once you're in a close position, you should obviously slow down. Remember that when there's one elk, there are usually more. I don't know how many times I've became so focused on a single animal, only moving when they put their head down to feed or are facing away, only to look up and see their unseen friend staring at me before bolting.

There are multiple approaches to sneaking in once you get close. Some remove their boots, and others use special covers like Cat's Paws, a felt-lined cover for the soles. I'm not a fan of either, as walking around in stocking feet always makes me nervous, and it never fails that the elk lead me farther and farther from my precious boots. I also hate all the movement required to remove them once you get in close. I'm normally too much of an ounce counter to justify packing around something like Cat's Paws, which don't serve multiple purposes. My best advice is to go slow and watch where you're putting your feet as you close the distance.

You can get away with a fair amount of movement, as long as elk are not directly looking at you. As with deer, elk really cannot pick you out if you remain still, even if they're staring right at you; if you think they've seen you, remain motionless until they lose interest. Keep in mind they'll often drop their heads only to snap them back up quickly to see if they'll catch you giving your presence away. Once they relax, you can continue your stalk.

Always use terrain to your advantage. If you have the opportunity to keep either hills, trees, or shrubs between you and your target, you'll be able to sneak in a lot closer than if you have to inch your way along.

### Decoys

Something I experienced firsthand several years ago changed in my mind forever about the importance of decoys. My dad and I we're dogging a small herd, trying to get the bull to come investigate our calls, but it was opening day in Colorado and that bull wanted to get his ladies out of there, as he was in no mood to deal with a satellite bull. As we were hurrying toward the sound of the last bugle, walking single file through the trees, I led us right past a cow at thirty yards. Talk about amateur hour! Of course she bolted. I was already holding my Montana butt decoy in my hand, so when the second cow bolted and got to the opening in the trees from which she could see us, I was already knelt down behind the decoy, and she stopped in her tracks. She stood in the opening for about thirty seconds, just staring at us, trying to figure out why the first cow had run, but after a few moments she started to calm down, and the rest of the herd went back to feeding.

After a couple minutes, I could have easily shot a cow, but the antler greed got the best of me when I saw a nice set bobbing through the trees. As the bull was heading for the same opening where the cows were, I came to full draw and stopped him perfectly at thirty yards. If it wasn't for an unbuckled chest strap from my pack hanging up my string and sending my arrow into space, that bull would have been packaged and in my freezer. It was another amateur move, but that's how hunting goes sometimes.

The point of the story is that the decoy turned what should have been a completely blown opportunity into what should have been a punched tag, and there are a couple noteworthy points to be made here:

Custom Carrying Case

1.  If that decoy hadn't already been in my hands, there is no way I could have deployed it in time. This year, I made a custom carrying case that hangs off my belt so I can pull the decoy out at a moment's notice.

2.  Because we were already moving and it was the second cow that saw the decoy, we were able to pull it off. I'd tried using decoys before, after already being busted, and they won't go for it, but used correctly, it was a great tool.

## Ambush

While sitting in a tree stand or ground blind over a game trail or wallow may not be my favorite method of elk hunting, it can be very effective. The key to this tactic is a solid understanding of the area in which you are hunting and animal movement from feeding to bedding areas to other areas within the day.

One of my favorite ambush spots is a thick stand of pines, where multiple trails converge between a couple high-country hay meadows and the elk bedding areas. I stumbled across this magical spot more out of dumb luck than anything. As I sat there staring at the intersection of three different trails, it dawned on me that it might be a good place to sit. The next day, from a quickly built ground blind, I had my bow drawn back six different times. Until then, I would have been happy to draw once during the course of a week-long hunt. That spot still calls to me many-an-opening-morning, as I know I'll likely be able to get a head start putting some meat in the freezer if I sit there.

I have swapped out my ground blind for a tree stand over the years, as I realized an elevated perch gives me a much better view of what is happening around me. Many times, it has provided those few extra seconds that have allowed me to get ready for the shot before the elk was right below me. In the areas where we hunt, elk are much less wary when it comes to looking for danger up in a tree, as compared to hunting whitetails out east, which seem to spend more time looking up than they do on the ground. Both the tree stand and the ground blind have their place in elk hunting. Weight is a consideration when going this route, however, as you'll likely be traveling farther than you would on a typical whitetail hunt, and you will have to carry your blind or stand with you to set it up.

Wallows are another great option for the ambush hunt. Personally, I don't like to use them unless I know for sure that they are getting hit hard. If it's obvious that the elk are coming in regularly, it may be just the ticket. Obvious signs would include water droplets still standing on the adjacent grass, muddy water, fresh tracks, etc.

It goes without saying that wind is a critical element in any ambush setup, as the mountain breezes often shift and swirl throughout the day. Finding consistent wind may be easier said than done.

Along with wallows come waterholes, and the terrain you're hunting will dictate whether sitting a waterhole is worthwhile or not. Water is plentiful in most of our spots, so sitting a waterhole obviously makes little sense. In drier climates, however, you can expect some animal visits at the local drink.

### Hunting Journal

My journey into writing really started by keeping a hunting journal. At first it was more of a field report: time, temperature, moon phase, animals spotted, etc. But, over the years, I became more involved with the local archery club, and they were always short of stories for the quarterly newsletter, so I offered to write a piece here and there, morphing the hunting journal into storytelling. Since then, I've really enjoyed trying to re-create our trips for readers to follow, offering something more than blow-by-blow accounts. The following hunt recap is from our 2008 trip to one of our favorite wilderness areas, when my diary first started to take on a little more than pure data collection.

To this day, as part of my opening day eve ritual, I pull out the old diary and thumb through the pages, hoping to recall just a tip or two from my own memory banks that may otherwise have resulted in another lesson from the School of Hard Knocks (or Nocks, as it were). While not necessarily a tactic, keeping notes on your hunt will force you to document what you are doing right or wrong, what you could do better or differently next time. Being able to go back to refresh yourself prior to heading to the field will help prevent you from making the same mistakes over and over. Many hunters only go hunting a handful of times a year, and out of those outings, we may only get one crack at a stalk or some type of encounter. If you can remember mistakes you've made in the past, chances are that much better you'll not make them again in the future.

## Hunting Journal - 2008 Bivy Hunt

Friday, September 12, 2008: I left town around one thirty p.m. and met Jeff's friend Nate ("SuperNacho") at Ted's Place at the mouth of the Poudre Canyon. Nate hadn't been up to our spot before, and it was tough to get back in there, so I volunteered to caravan up with him. Some snow was spitting on the drive up, and the mountain passes had several inches on the ground already; it was looking like it might be a tough trip!

When we got to the trailhead, Big Ron's truck was there, but he wasn't around, which meant he was running a load of gear up the trail on the four-wheeler. We hung out for a little bit while another afternoon shower blew through. It was definitely looking like I might be in for a long week.

We got up to camp after dark and set up my tent in the rain. We had a few beers with the fellas and went to bed.

Loading up at the Trailhead

Saturday, September 13 (Full moon, 65-70 degrees, clear skies): Woke up at five a.m. Drew and I were the only ones to make it out of camp early, and we were planning on staying out for five days with our bivy gear. By the way, after adding a few odds and ends my pack, water, bow and all weighed in at fifty-five pounds. As we were walking out of camp, we noticed three muzzleloader hunters heading in the same direction as we were. They ended up getting in front of us, which was fine. That way, we could see which way they were headed and hunt someplace else.

Drew with a Full Pack

But as soon as we got to the big meadow outside of the old horse camp, we heard elk crashing through the trees. Since we've encountered elk here many times, we had a pretty good idea which way they were heading and took off running, hoping to keep ahead of them. We heard the muzzleloaders bugling to the elk and had to laugh because we knew they didn't have a chance. We only know this because we'd been outsmarted at that very spot too many times. It turned out that we lucked out and made the right call.

When we approached the knob after jogging about one and a half miles, it was incredible. We heard about 6 bulls all bugling within 200 yards. I sat back to call for Drew and called in a small raghorn that came to within forty-five yards. While I was waiting for Drew to shoot, it seems we miscommunicated, and he was off chasing one of the other five bulls, which he never caught up with.

I captured some video of the bull and wondered where Drew had gone, as the elk seemed to quiet down a bit. Drew returned after a while, and we sat down to relax with a hot cup of coffee and some granola. Afterward, we heard a few more bugles, which gave us an idea which direction the elk were headed, so we grabbed our stuff and kept following.

Around midday, we stopped for lunch, but Drew wanted to continue another 400 to 500 yards up the hill, and I was going to call again, hoping a bull would respond while he was close enough to sneak in. I'm not sure what happened, but I didn't see Drew for another couple hours. Apparently, he saw thirty-five to forty-five elk during that time and almost had a couple shots, but it never panned out.

Toward the end of the afternoon, we climbed out of the bowl we'd hunted all morning and saw another sixteen elk on the adjacent hillside. There was a fairly nice bull with the bunch. We ended up getting to within about thirty yards of that bull before I got busted; I just happened to get caught out in the open as he popped out of the trees and got a good look at me. It was pretty disappointing since he would have been a great bull, and it had been a great stalk up to that point.

We set up bivy camp on the hillside that night about four to five miles from where we started out that morning. Drew wanted to give one last bugle before calling it a night, and wouldn't you know he called to a bull within thirty yards of our sleeping bags? The elk sang us to sleep that night, and we couldn't have asked for a better day.

*Sunday, September 14:* Since the elk had been bugling all night and had woken us up multiple times, we had a pretty good idea where to head in the morning. As we were trying to get ready, we heard a bull bugling within about 200 yards of camp, so we got dressed as quickly and quietly as possible. We ended up getting into a herd of about ten cows, a herd bull, and several satellite bulls and dogged the herd down the side of the mountain before they lost us.

After all the excitement that morning, we headed back to our bivy camp for coffee and breakfast: granola, powered milk, and protein powder for me, and dehydrated Mountain House eggs, ham, and green peppers for Drew. His looked better than my granola mix, and I made a mental note to add some variety for breakfast next year. We also dropped down to a natural spring to refill our water supply.

We were able to get hold of Big Ron on the radio around ten that morning and talked him into heading out to bivy with us. He ended up showing up later that afternoon.

That night, we returned to where we'd lost the herd

Drew and Big Ron

earlier that morning but didn't have any luck. They finally started bugling after dark, and we thought one was going to walk right up to us. It was pretty cool to sit there in the moonlight listening to the bulls bugle.

*Monday, September 15:* Woke up at six a.m. and packed up our bivys. We gave a few locate bugles off the top of the mountain, trying to determine which direction to travel. We heard a couple bugles from the triple-nipple to the north and a single bugle down the mountain to the west. Since heading west would keep us closer to base camp, that was the direction we decided go to. Of course, when we got to the bottom of the mountain, he quit bugling, so we sat down around nine thirty for some breakfast and to figure out a new game plan. As we were screwing around boiling water for coffee and jabbering away, I saw a couple cows walking through the trees about forty-five yards away. I told Drew to cow call, grabbed my bow, and headed toward them. Unfortunately, I think they were wise to our mid-mountain breakfast buffet and ran out of there.

About the same time, we heard another bugle from the bull that had brought us down the mountain that morning, but he was getting further and further away. Big Ron and I decided to stay put and keep calling while Drew took off after him. The plan worked great until we called in another hunter; it was another reminder to practice our calls, as his calling was absolutely

horrendous, and we knew it wasn't an elk long before he showed up.

We decided to walk a couple miles and sit for a few hours in an elky-looking area before the evening bulging hopefully picked back up

Bivy Camp

again. As we were sitting, we decide to cook an early dinner, since we would likely hunt until right before dark. As we were boiling water for a dehydrated meal, elk started to bugle, and one seemed to be getting closer. We quickly finished up and headed toward the nearest bugle, which wasn't far off. As it turned out, the bull was bugling from a big wallow, raking the tress with his antlers. All three of us were watching from about fifty yards away when a second, larger elk showed up and ran him out of the wallow.

Big Ron had been bugling, which kept both of the elk fired up, and Drew took off chasing them. We talked to him on the radio about a half-hour later, and he told us he'd shot a bull. We went to help him track the bull and were lucky that he hadn't gone too far. We all worked in the dark by headlamp, skinning, boning, and hanging the elk meat to cool.

*Tuesday, September 16:* We knew it was going to be a long day, because it was

five miles to the nearest four-wheeler trail. Those 5 miles included a 1,000-foot vertical descent through some nasty blow-down, followed by several miles of half-flat wilderness trail and a couple tough miles with another 1,000-foot climb back to the top. Worst of all, it was going to take two

Big Ron, Drew, and Me after Drew's Kill

trips. The first trip Drew and I packed half our bivy gear and a sack of boned-out elk meat, a total of eighty to ninety pounds a piece. Big Ron packed out all his bivy gear and the antlers.

After the first five miles, Big Ron headed down another trail back to base camp to get the four-wheeler, and Drew and I dropped back down for another load of meat and the rest of our gear.

Drew in His Bivy

We ended up crawling out of the bowl at about eight thirty that night by headlamp, sweating and dragging, having walked fifteen miles that day with heavy loads. It was brutal! Big Ron had dropped off a four-wheeler, a few cold beers, and burritos, quite possibly the best thing we'd ever seen.

*Wednesday, September 17*: I slept in, then woke up and screwed around camp, drinking coffee and eating breakfast burritos. We packed up and headed down the trail by eleven a.m. Other than some awfully sore legs, we had an unbelievable trip.

On a side note, we talked to a lot of guys on the trails. Nobody had seen any elk or heard any bugles, even though we'd had the best trip of our lives. It just goes to show that a little boot leather can go a long way in elk country!

Packing Out

# Shot Placement

I've broken this chapter into two sections, rifle and archery. Broadhead tipped arrows are no match for heavy bone and must be placed precisely to quickly bring down these big, tough animals. Riflemen, on the other hand, can be more

THE ELK

opportunistic, taking straight-on and severe quartering shots. Where bullets are capable of shattering bone, even those wielding rifles should take the time to understand basic anatomy to hone their skills and refine their shot placement.

Every hunter dreams of the shot where the animal's head is down, body slightly quartering away, with his front leg extended slightly forward, but in my experience, you'll spend a lot of time in the woods before you'll encounter this magical combination. Most encounters happen quickly, and if you have a solid understanding of the animal's anatomy, you'll be able to entertain different options with your shot placement and won't always be forced to wait for that elusive perfect shot.

Mr. Zach Sanders's recommendations on shot placement do not necessarily follow conventional advice; I'd also remind the reader that Zach is an accomplished marksman and taking such shots may not be for everyone. Regardless of your weapon, it's up to you, as an individual, to determine what shot you can confidently take. What's right for one individual may not be for everyone.

### Rifle (by Zach Sanders)

**Head/Neck/Central Nervous System:** If you are not concerned with the trophy aspect of the animal and are confident that you can deliver a well-placed headshot, go for it. It will anchor the animal exactly where they are standing and makes blood trailing a non-issue. Be warned: A bad headshot can be a sickening experience. The neck shot is sometimes difficult on elk, unlike deer. When shooting a deer in the neck, many people don't hit the spinal column at all, but the shock of the bullet impacting the animal breaks the neck, and the desired result is achieved. If you want to try neck shots, you should look into the specific anatomy of an elk to better understand where the spine is located.

**Heart/Lung:** A heart shot ensures a fast, clean kill. The heart on an elk is located below center of the body horizontally, slightly behind the front leg when observed broadside. The lung shot is my personal favorite, the shot I recommend when circumstances allow. The lungs are the largest vital organs; when destroyed, it incapacitates the animal quickly. When aiming at the lungs, shoot for center and just behind the front shoulder of an animal standing broadside. This will minimize the amount of meat ruined from the shot and increase the odds of a kill if your bullet placement is a little off. If you are aiming for the lungs and your bullet strikes low, there is a good chance you will hit the heart; if it hits high, you might hit the spine; and if the bullet drifts forward, you may hit the shoulder. If the bullet is heavy enough to break through the scapula, you may still have a lung hit.

Keep in mind the relative position of the organs you aim to puncture as the elk presents different body positions to you and where the bullet will have to strike the hide to achieve your desired results. For example: If the elk is quartering away, you will need to fire somewhere in the vicinity of the last rib closest to the hind quarters for the bullet to find its way through the center of the chest cavity and hopefully both lungs.

## Archery

Archers need to remember that broadheads kill by either cutting major arteries or organs, creating massive hemorrhaging, or by collapsing the lungs, pneumothorax. Elk are tough, tough animals that do not let go of life without a fight, and shots need to be precise to put them down quickly. Because they are large animals with a generous vital area, some hunters believe they have a greater margin of error, but arrows that are not placed within that sweet spot (heart/lungs) will result in impossible blood trails and unrecovered animals.

## Pick-a-Spot

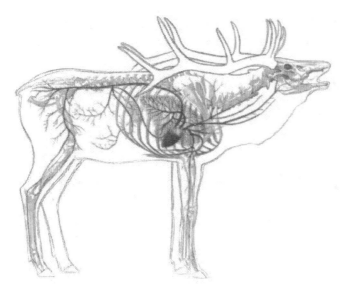

It may seem that elk are so big that it's impossible to miss, but I assure you that is not the case. Executing a shot comes down to how much practice you've put in at the range preseason.

Even then, shooting at a foam broadside elk target while you joke around with your buddies is nothing like shooting at a big bull that is right there screaming in your face. Imagine this scenario: You've crept to within seventy or eighty yards of a big herd bull and all his cows. As you're waiting to figure out your next move, he begins pushing the cows directly toward you. The cows somehow part around you, until you are surrounded by them ten yards on either side, with the big boy crossing side to side behind them. You're just waiting for the wind to swirl and everything to blow up in your face, and you're not really sure how you made it that far. As the big bull makes another push, you realize it's now or never. If you're not a ball of nerves by that point, you need a more adrenaline-packed hobby, like skydiving or bungee jumping!

The most important advice I can give in regard to buck/bull fever is to concentrate on going through the same steps you do at the range. Specifically make sure you've found your anchor, picked the right pin, picked a spot, and that you are relaxed enough to execute a smooth release.

I believe more elk are lost each year to shots that are either too high or too far back. If you look at the diagrams above, you'll notice that a center body shot will result in hitting the top of the lungs; while this may be lethal, an elk may travel a long way before death, and the blood trail can be minimal. My advice is to subtract approximately eight inches from the top of an elk's back, then divide the remainder of the body in half and aim for that point, either directly up the front leg or slightly behind for a broadside shot; if it's anything other than broadside, aim for the far leg. In bowhunter education, I was taught to aim for the middle of the animal, the theory being that this would give me the most room for error if the yardage was misjudged. The reason I feel this advice is flawed is that the top six to eight inches of an elk is void of any critical arterial systems. While a true spine shot will drop an animal in its tracks, a hit above the spine will only result is superficially blood loss.

For those interested in a more in-depth study of anatomy, I always recommend looking at the skeletal structure beneath the skin; it's easiest to see this when animals are in their summer coats. Remember that most four-legged critters share the same bone structure. If you don't have an elk handy, deer, horses, cows, and other animals all exhibit similar skeletal structures. I believe many are misinformed about where the shoulder blade actually lies within the body, thinking it follows the legs directly up. In fact, the scapula and humerous angle toward the front of the animal, leaving the heart and all connecting arteries wide open. The more one studies anatomy, the better your opportunity for kill shots will be.

The included Elk anatomy guides may be obtained from the National Bowhunter Education Foundation at www.nbef.org

# Blood Trailing

I don't know why, but I truly enjoy working out the clues of a good blood trail. Maybe it's because I know all my hard work and preparation is about to pay off. Elk that have been well hit in the heart or lungs are fairly simple to locate. The other shots, however, can make blood trailing far more interesting and difficult.

This bull traveled over 1.5 miles before being put down.

There are some tips worth keeping in mind. First, even with a well placed arrow, it's not uncommon for elk to travel 100 to 150 yards or more. Depending on where the animal was hit, the blood trail may be minimal, as the body cavity is filling up with blood but only small amounts are hitting the ground. Just be paitent and do your best to stay on the tracks. The other thing that is always surpriszing to those new to blood trailing is the amount of blood that can be lost. It's amazing how much blood can be on the ground, yet the animal is still never found.

First, don't trust your eyes. We've been on a lot of blood trails (most not our own, thank goodness) over the years, and whenever we come across the stranger in the field who looks slightly confused, scratching his head and crawling around on hands and knees, the story always starts with, "I made a great shot and...well, maybe just a little high or far back." Elk are big, tough critters that can go a long way; they may even completely recover if they are not hit in the heart or lungs.

Immediately after taking the shot, it's important to remain composed and watch the animal until it runs out of sight. Why blood trail if you don't have to? When watching, take special note as to where the animal was standing when it was hit, its direction of travel, and where it was last seen. After watching the animal depart, immediately mark the spot where you stood to take the shot, either by sticking an arrow in the ground or using fluorescent surveyor's (marking) tape. Many times, it's helpful to go back to this spot and use it as a point of reference if you have trouble locating the downed animal.

Next, investigate where the animal was standing when it was hit. Obviously, if you saw the animal run off with your arrow sticking out of its side, you won't be looking for the arrow or the point of impact, but many times, hunters are unsure of their shots, not knowing

Another reason sharp broadheads are a must!

exactly where the animal was hit, or even if it was hit at all. In these situations, you should either find blood or your arrow. If you missed, you should be able to locate your arrow and confirm no blood and go back to your hunt; if you cannot, chances are that the animal ran off with it, so you should be able to find blood. Either way, you should be able to find one or the other.

Here's where being able to go back to your shooting point comes into play. Determine where the animal was last standing and mark that spot. Then go back to the shot, line up the angles, and you may be able to discern what happened. On last year's hunt, one of our guys was pretty sure he'd missed a shot but wasn't 100 percent sure. With the standing rule, blood or arrow, five of us spent several hours combing the ground on hands and knees. Finally, someone noticed a tiny patch of missing bark on a tree where a blade from the broadhead had scraped the trunk. A few minutes later, we found the arrow about twelve feet up a spruce tree, with no blood on the shaft, so we went back to hunting.

Once you do find your arrow, it will provide you with clues as to where the animal was hit. Bright pink, frothy blood with tiny air bubbles indicates a lung hit, while green and foul-smelling would indicate a gut shot. Solid red, dark blood is said to indicate a muscle hit. Your arrow (or what's left of it) can also give you an indication of penetration. My favorite is a pass-through with the shaft completely covered in blood. The very first cow I shot with a bow (and did not recover) resulted in a shoulder hit, which I knew when the arrow hit her and almost immediately stopped. When I found my arrow with only the tip broken off, and that confirmed what my eyes had seen. I'm quite certain that cow lived to see another day.

Archers should always wait a minimum of forty-five minutes before taking up the blood trail. You want to make sure the animal has time to expire, or you risk the chance of pushing them, creating a lot more work for yourself and greatly reducing the odds of recovery. Anything other than a textbook shot requires a greater wait time. Typically, it's advised that gut shot animals be given a minimum of six hours before you take up the trail. When blood trailing, scan the area ahead to make sure the animals isn't bedded down, watching their back-trail.

Many times there will only be a few specks of blood at the point of impact, which can be very difficult to find. Don't forget to look for other clues like hair cut by a razor-sharp broadhead or where the ground was torn up when the animal bolted. When an elk is hit and takes off running, the terrain will look like a heavy equipment work zone. It can be much more challenging if the elk was part of a herd, as you'll have many tracks to sort through. Finding blood is key in this scenario. Remember that the animal you're after will not be able to keep up with the others and will, at some point, pull away from the herd.

On more difficult blood trails, one trick we utilize is to determine the stride of an animal. Typically, blood is forced off of the body or wound with each step. Once you determine the distance between steps, you can fairly accurately judge where the next blood should be. We cut a tree branch to the length of the animal's supposed stride and use it as an indicator, placing it on the last blood spot and extending it in the anticipate direction of travel. Many times, this technique helps you find that elusive next spot and keeps you moving forward.

You owe it to the animal and yourself to exhaust every effort and keep looking until the animal is found. Don't give up until you do!

## Meat Care

Once an animal hits the ground, there's nothing more important than getting them broken down as quickly and cleanly as possible. Whether you plan on bringing your animal out on your back, a game cart, or hiring a packer to help you do the job, you'll still need to do some planning. There are a couple obvious tools you'll need, regardless of which method you choose: a sharp knife and sharpener, game bags, and rope (I prefer 550 Paracord).

**Trophy Photos**

Don't forget to get your pictures before you break out your knife!

- Remove brush from around the face and head.
- Wipe away excessive blood and tuck the tongue back in the mouth.
- Rearrange or reposition the animal if necessary.
- Take lots of photos, which is especially easy with digital cameras. Vary the angles and use both flash and no flash to ensure that you get the perfect trophy shot.

## Knives

Knives seem to be a very personal choice for many hunters, but almost anything will work as long as the person doing the cutting knows what he or she is doing and the blade is nice and sharp. If using the gutless method, a three-inch blade is all that's required to get your animal broken down and into game bags.

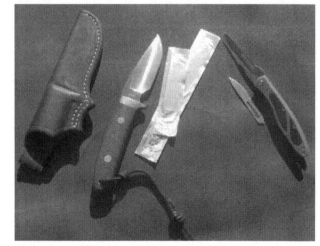

My personal preference is a combination of different styles of knives. One is a custom knife made by a local knife maker, Wayne Depperschmidt. It is constructed of high-grade steel and will hold an edge (with careful cutting, avoiding hair, bone, etc.) through an entire elk or two without requiring sharpening or touching up. While many prefer to carry a small sharpening stone or steel in the field, I've never found it necessary. I always carry a secondary knife, the Havalon Piranta, with a couple replacement blades. These are amazingly sharp, so I take extra time with them in the field. They cut through muscle like butter and are great for caping.

I should mention that the custom knife I carry is my lucky one, and while it is a handy tool, I carry it more out of nostalgia and superstition than anything. Most of the other hunters in my crew use Leathermans almost exclusively for quartering and skinning just about anything with four legs, and it obviously has all the other tools that can prove to be invaluable in a backcountry setting as well. As I said before, knives are a very personal choice, as long as it is sharp and you know how to handle it safely so that the only thing you're butchering is your animal.

Saws are not required all the time, as antlers can be removed with a knife by removing the entire skull, down to the lower jaw. This all depends on what you intend to do with the antlers. You may only be concerned about getting the antlers out for legal reasons (many states have minimum point requirements), and Colorado also requires that the skull plate not be broken or the antlers separated from the skull plate until out of the filed. Skullcapping is the quickest and easiest method but does require the use of a saw. This can be a fairly gruesome procedure for someone who is not used to carving up big game animals. The first cut is made starting behind the antlers, at the top of the head, angled down through the eye socket. A second cut is made in front of the antlers, again aiming for the eye socket. I'm a fan of the Wyoming saws for this procedure if this is something you're considering.

## Game Bags

Never leave camp without them! This requires a little positive thinking, but get in the habit of buying them in bulk! I hate the idea of having to go back to camp before breaking down an animal, and these bags are

Getting the meat off the ground so air can circulate is critical to help with a faster cool-down to prevent spoiling.

lightweight and don't take up much room in the pack. Leaving them behind doesn't make any sense, since taking care of game meat should be the number one priority when an animal goes down. Having a game bag ready to go is a no-brainer.

I've been using Allen game bags with no complaints and have never lost any meat due to bag failure; these are now being sold under the Remington brand at Walmart. I have heard horror stories about lesser quality bags, specifically when the weave is more open, as this allows flies to lay eggs through the fabric, resulting in meat loss.

## Gutless Method

If you've never heard of the gutless method and are still gutting animals, you need to pay attention to this section. We use to handle field dressing animals much the same way our grandfathers did, which started by gutting, but now I almost never go that route.

In my opinion, the gutless method is much easier, cleaner, and quicker. The only reason to gut an animal would be to get at the heart and liver, and even then, the gutless method can be employed first. Those organs can be removed at the end of the process.

There really isn't a right or wrong way to skin, quarter, or gut any animal, and every hunter seems to do things a little differently. Regardless of how you go about the process, there are a couple basic things to keep in mind as you're working on an animal. First, you should try to minimize the amount of dirt and hair that gets on the meat. Be very careful about the placement of your feet as you move around to work on the animal; it is very easy in some conditions to kick dirt up on the skinned meat. Second, fold the skin back only a section at a time and use it to act as a tarp to place the meat on as it is removed. Always keep the hair side to the ground and place the meat on the inside of the hide.

If you're planning on caping the animal, skin the area you'll be taking for the cape (typically all the skin from the head down to several inches past the armpits) prior to starting the following steps:

1. Start by skinning the animal on one side. Starting from the front leg, skin up the leg, through the brisket, up to the spine. The next cut will follow the belly toward the rear quarter.

2. Remove the front shoulder. By lifting the leg and cutting the connective tissue along the ribs, the leg will easily separate from the body.

3. Remove the rear quarter. This is the same process as the front quarter, but you'll need to follow the pelvic bone and cut along the ball joint on the underside of the leg. Then, working from the topside, cut along the hip bone and remove any remaining meat to separate the quarter. Remember to leave evidence of sex if this is a requirement in the area you are hunting.

4. Remove the backstrap by following the spine down to the ribs and along the underside of the backstrap.

5. Remove neck, brisket, and flank meat.

6. People often ask how to get to the tenderloins without gutting. At the last rib, push down on the belly area of the elk to expose the tenderloins. It is sometimes helpful to poke a small hole in the body cavity to relieve any bloating.

7. Roll the animal over and repeat on the other side.

There are many videos online describing this procedure in a much clearer way than I can with written words. A good one can be found at Elk101.com - http://elk101.com/videos/gutless-video/.

Place each quarter in a game bag as it's removed from the animal, then place the bags in the shade. Once all the meat is in game bags it should be hung from a tree to allow air circulation all the way around the bag. Look for the shadiest tree you can find, taking note which direction the sun is moving to try to anticipate a good amount of shade throughout the day. Branches can be removed from surrounding trees to help shade your hanging spot. Also take care to use sticks as spacers anywhere where the quarters want to rest on the trunk of the tree or against each other. Again, you want to maximize circulation to the entire surface area of the quarter to promote quick cooling.

### To Quarter or De-Bone?

Our personal preference is typically to quarter our animals, though distance from the vehicle dictates whether we will do that or de-bone. There are definitely pros and cons to each method. De-boning obviously shaves a couple pounds off your pack weight and allows meat to cool quicker, since you're reducing the mass and thermal transfer rate. However, by opening up the

---

[3] Photos courtesy of Corey Jacobsen and Rikki Swedhin

quarters, you create a greater surface area on the meat, which can get dirty and be exposed to insects. We also typically prefer to pack a solid quarter that can be cinched down tight to the pack vs. a bag of meat that wants to work its way into the bottom of your pack.

**Storage and Packing**

Field conditions will dictate how you'll manage your meat once it's been properly bagged and cooled. If temperatures are extremely high, in the seventies and eighties and nights are only dropping to the low thirties, you'll want to get your meat to a cooler (meat locker) in the first couple days. When hunting in the later seasons or when temperatures are cooler, your meat will be fine hanging for the duration of your hunt.

I personally like to let my quarters hang through the night; even in the early archery seasons, it can be in the mid-thirties. Then, after it cools all night to ambient temperatures, I throw it in the cooler and either get it to a meat locker or head to the house to start my own butchering.

Regardless of how or what you do with your game meat, remember what it took to get to this point. Not only does my elk feed my family for the year, but I believe the elk gods smile upon those who make the most of their harvest.

# Additional Resources

This book is intended to be a starting place for the new hunter, but there is no better resource than the World Wide Web, a truly amazing source of information.

## Elk Calling

There are two resources I recommend to anyone interested in learning more about calling.

### Elknut Outdoor Productions - http://www.elknut.com/

I owe a lot of our success to Paul Medel, the Elknut. If you're interest in learning what those elk are saying, I'd highly recommend checking out the Elknut site. His calling CDs and DVDs are highly informative and describe the vocalizations in much greater detail than I've described in these pages. If you truly want to enhance your time spent in the field as well as your success, you owe it to yourself to check them out. Don't be penny-wise and pound foolish! If you consider how much money is tied up in an elk hunt (licenses, fuel, food, lodging, gear, etc.), a couple extra dollars on education about vocalizations is money well spent. My only word of caution is that they produce videos for education, not entertainment. If you want a Primos-type elk hunting video, this is not the place to go.

### Roe Hunting Resources - http://roehuntingresources.com/

I first learned about Chris Roe after we'd been listening to Elknut for several years. At that point, we were starting to regularly fill tags, to the point where I thought, *What could I possibly learn from this guy?* I'm very glad I took the time to hear what he was talking about. Chris has a degree in wildlife biology and spent several college summers living on the side of a mountain studying elk behavior and vocalizations. After just a few minutes of listening to him, you'll know he knows his stuff! I really think his information complements Elknut's well. Their assessments are not always the same, so I like to compare what each of them has to offer to what I've experienced in the field and draw my own conclusions from there. If you want to take your understanding of vocalizations and behavior to the next level, you owe it to yourself to check out Roe Hunting Resources.

## Online Forums and Etiquette

I think the younger generation has a better grasp of this than those who didn't grow up in an online world. Online hunting forums can be a tremendous resource; however, there are a few basic rules to learn before making your first post. Online forums are not for everyone, and while I'm guilty of having a hard time staying off of them, I know most my hunting partners are the exactly opposite.

1. Take some time to learn to navigate any new site. If applicable, look for any search buttons that may lead you to the answer you seek before asking for help.
2. Don't be the guy that asks, "So...I'm thinking about heading out to hunt. Where should I start looking? I don't want anyone's honey holes, just a general area with an opportunity to kill any animal." This is basically what everyone is looking for. As with speaking with the biologist, ask for specifics, do your homework, and you'll likely get better responses.
3. Be aware that good elk hunting grounds are hard earned. Most would rather sell their firstborn before giving up their elk spots, let alone be foolish enough to post specifics on the Web. Many sites have private messaging features; use those to talk to other hunters one on one. You'll likely get to know someone better, and they may be willing to help you out.
4. Beware of misinformation! I know I break into a cold sweat whenever I see the name of any of our hunting areas posted on the Web, and I'm sure I'm not the only one. Expect that not all the responses will be genuine, and some may only be trying to get you to look somewhere else.

**Bowsite - http://www.bowsite.com/bowsite/home/**

One of my personal favorites and something I read as regularly as the morning paper is Bowsite, which has forums dedicated strictly to elk hunting, those dedicated to many other species, and state-specific forums. There are many extremely experienced guys on the site who are very willing to help and provide the most accurate and up-to-date information. In the state-specific forums, you can get in touch with those in your local archery community and find information specific to your state. It's a great resource if you're looking for local 3-D shoots or a hunting partner wanting to split gas for an out-of-state hunt.

**Elk101- http://elk101.com/**

Corey Jacobson, eight-time world champion elk caller, shares his passion for elk hunting on his website, which includes forums, articles, videos, as well as in his magazine, *Extreme Elk*. These are both great resources for those looking for additional information regarding elk hunting.

## RokSlide - http://www.rokslide.com/

This site is dedicated to the DIY Western hunters. Most of the content is backpacker/hiking specific, and those running the site are as dedicated as it gets when it comes to backcountry adventure. If you're into this type of hunting, you'll likely find their forums and articles to be very helpful.

## Rocky Mountain Elk Foundation (RMEF) - http://www.rmef.org/

RMEF is dedicated to conservation, habitat preservation, and acquisition of land for elk. I'd encourage anyone who enjoys elk hunting to join and give support to ensure the future of our sport for generations to come.

## Hardcore Outdoor - http://www.hardcoreoutdoor.com/

I enjoy this site for keeping current with the latest technologies regarding technical clothing, optics, footwear, etc. The author is a highly regarded outdoorsman and is dedicated to reviewing gear without bias. My only word of caution is that his focus is best in class, the best of the best, so if you're on a tight budget, you'll likely not find much in your spending range. I do believe in spending as much as you can afford for quality gear, but that number varies greatly for each of us. I have found typically with higher quality gear you get what you pay for and you won't need to replace items after only a couple years of use. And remember you'll be trusting your gear to keep you warm and comfortable, which may translate into alive in the many backcountry environments. I'd suggest spending as much as you can afford when it comes to sleeping, shelter, and quality outdoor clothing.

## Colorado Parks and Wildlife - http://wildlife.state.co.us/Pages/Home.aspx

Online resources vary from state to state, but Colorado has done a great job helping new hunters. They offer a wealth of information on everything from the basics to draw odds, and I've already mentioned the benefits of their interactive mapping.

Made in the USA
Lexington, KY
03 March 2015